A CANADIAN PEOPLE

"*There is only one thing worse than Injustice, and that is Justice without her sword in her hand.*"

OSCAR WILDE.

"*Justice without Force is powerless. Force without Justice is tyrannical. Let us therefore unite Force and Justice, and have it so that whatever is strong, shall be just, and whatever is just, shall be strong.*"

BLAISE PASCAL.

"*Canada can never be quite like her neighbour, and that is all to the good, for it means that she has a specific contribution of her own to make to North American civilization. I like to think of her, with her English and French peoples, as in a special degree the guardian of the great Mediterranean tradition which descends from Greece and Rome, and which she has to mould to the uses of a new world. I want to see her keep her individuality, for that is of inestimable advantage, not only to her, but to her neighbour.*"

LORD TWEEDSMUIR.

A CANADIAN PEOPLE

LORNE PIERCE

Toronto ~ The Ryerson Press

Designed by Thoreau MacDonald

ACKNOWLEDGMENT

Chapters II and III first appeared
in *The Canadian Spokesman*, April
and May, 1941, and were issued as
Beverley Paper V in the same year.

THE BEVERLEY PAPERS

I. TOWARD THE BONNE ENTENTE (1929)

II. UNEXPLORED FIELDS OF CANADIAN LITERATURE (1932)

III. THREE FREDERICTON POETS (1933)

IV. J. E. H. MacDONALD: A POSTSCRIPT (1940)

V. THE ARMOURY IN OUR HALLS (1941)

VI. THOREAU MacDONALD (1942)

VII. MARJORIE PICKTHALL (1943)

VIII. "PRIME MINISTERS TO THE BOOK" (1944)

IX. A CANADIAN PEOPLE (1945)

PRINTED AND BOUND IN CANADA

To

BETH AND BRUCE

The Fifth Generation

FOREWORD

THIS small book contains the gist of what I have
been trying to say for a long time about Canada.
A Canadian of the fourth generation, I have been
devoted to all that concerns my country—its traditions,
its latent wealth, and its destiny—and have dedicated
myself to Canada with an affection which some have
thought bordered upon fanaticism. For a quarter of
a century, both as writer and editor, I have endeav-
oured to interpret Canada honestly to itself and explain
it candidly to others. I have tried unceasingly to
build a covered bridge between East and West,
between Catholic and Protestant, between French
and English, in the hope that our nation might be
invincible. I have sought to honour the real architects
of our future greatness—the creative artists and
writers of the Dominion. And I have implored our
people, year in and year out, to grow up, to have the
courage to be themselves. Looking back it all seems
quite futile.

So far as I am aware, no book has been published
by the mother publishing house of Canada, of which
I have been for so long a time the editor, that has
failed to represent, both in letter and in spirit, one
or other of those wistful objectives. Across the entire
list of this great House, in history, biography and
travel, belles lettres, fiction and poetry, commentaries
upon our arts and letters, public, high school and
university texts, pamphlets and encyclopædias, in all

these, season after season, I have stressed it again and again.

The situation in Canada has steadily gone from bad to worse. The more we talk beautifully about the *entente cordiale* the more vicious we become. Yet it has seemed right to set down once and for all what I believe, and with all the energy I possess. Our public relations in Canada are so disturbing, the whole idea of confederation so dreadfully endangered, that men of vision and good will must move now or never. Have we intelligence enough to stop short of the wicked ultimate? Must we yet await an outside authority to decide for us at some Senlac Hill? Shall we give madness the rein and go on to some Culloden or Gettysburg? Can we find in all this land one hundred English and one hundred French who will believe in each other, in honour prefer one another, and, come hell or high water, champion the other? They will save the nation. We may take the road that will lead to the status of one of the first progressive powers of the earth, a tower of strength, a beacon of light. Or we may take another road, one that will bring us to a place among those bankrupt states, decadent and reactionary, the very refuse of the world, too petty to hate, too trivial to scorn.

LORNE PIERCE.

York Mills, Ontario
March 1, 1945

CONTENTS

PAGE

FOREWORD vii

CHAPTER

I. OUR INTELLECTUAL SABOTEURS . 1

II. THE ARMOURY IN OUR HALLS . 7
    1. THE WILL TO BE FREE . . . 7
    2. THE WILL TO BE OURSELVES . . 9
    3. THE WITNESS OF HISTORY . . 12

III. OUR INVINCIBLE LEADERS . . 16
    1. THE LEADERSHIP OF THE ÉLITE . . 17
    2. HISTORIANS AND THE PEOPLE . . 18
    3. LITERATURE AND LIFE . . . 21
    4. FREE MEN IN A FREE DEMOCRACY . 25

IV. REHEARSAL FOR SUICIDE . . 30
    1. RITUAL FOR DEATH 30
    2. A SHROUD FOR CULTURE . . . 34
    3. THE BATTLE OF SLOGANS . . . 36
    4. THE CULT OF FEAR 43
    5. GOVERNMENT BY BLACKMAIL . . 48

V. A CANADIAN PEOPLE . . . 53

A Canadian People

I

OUR INTELLECTUAL SABOTEURS

THIS is an attempt to gather up the writer's ideas
and prejudices about Canada, more especially
concerning the Canadian people—the possibility of
building a nation here at all; if so, the hope of a working *bonne entente* between French and English. What
prospect have we of creating a soul beneath the ribs
of death, a living faith, so that we may survive as a
people, a strong people, strongly individualized and
useful to mankind?

I offer the proposition, that the so-called intellectuals
of Canada have been its real saboteurs, that these
rodents had so undermined the foundations of the
state, and the bastions of its main defence, that, when
danger at last threatened our very existence, we
reached out, and lo, there was nothing to lay hold
upon. The farmer, the labourer and the little man
have been nearer the truth than the pale theorists and
the florid big shots. They see the necessity for a
strongly united Canada, and for an indestructible
British Commonwealth, for they see man living on
the edge of the jungle, with a lot of the ape, the tiger
and the boa-constrictor still in his veins, where to be
secure at all means that all men of like faith and of

1

good will must hold together absolutely in all weathers. High school teachers, university men, editors, political adventurers and others in surprising numbers have been saying, for a long time, that the British Empire was washed up, that it was morally bankrupt, and that Confederation would collapse from dry rot, and even now was crumbling and decaying before our eyes. This Dominion, just before 1939 and the time of the winnowing of nations, had sunk to a new all-time low, sunk into a state of moral coma, spiritual fibrillation, and political paralysis, not different in any essential respect from demoralized France before her incredible and humiliating fall.

Returning from Europe, in 1934, I told everyone I met that a tornado was thundering out of the East. The thing I saw through Europe, up the Rhine and down the Danube, made me physically ill. The fear and suspicion, in the little countries; the pent up hate and cold malice and will for revenge as you moved toward Munich, Vienna and Budapest. On their monuments were simple placards hung by twine about the necks of their heroes in marble in the public squares, and the words were—"No! No! Never!"

In Vienna, the day after Dolfuss was liquidated, and in the hotel that became the fortress of the Gastapo and the temporary prison of Schuschnigg, an Austrian lawyer and former Captain of a crack cavalry regiment, a man whose mother had been lady-in-waiting to the Empress, told me that everyone could see something was on the way. Personally he thought nothing could be worth more bloodshed, but the desperation of millions was only waiting for the right kind of opportunity. And it happened to come through

2

a Vienna house-painter! When I returned from Budapest and entered beautiful Graz, a jewel among its overhanging mountains, gangs of guerrillas were even then shooting it out in the hills around the city, and the situation getting quite out of hand in Europe. As I moved down through the Brenner Pass into Italy the arrogance of countless marching Nazi youths was matched in every mountain hamlet by the insolence of unnumbered strutting Fascist youths. Where did they all come from, and for what? Before the Millennial Monument in Budapest, a magnificent colonnade dedicated to a thousand years of Magyar rule, endless streams of people, young and old, paused all day long, bowed and muttered a confession of faith that went like this: "I believe in God; I believe in truth; I believe justice will prevail. Amen." Something was bound to happen, the top blow off, if drastic remedies were not tried in a hurry. But the enlightened nations slept.

One of the incredible facts of history is this: the amazing blindness, deafness, dumbness and paralysis of our own people, of the Empire and the United States, during those fatal years. I roared with rage at the sight, but the best my friends could advise was that I keep cool. It became the smart thing to ridicule England for her lack of leadership. Flying over the Rockies one day, in 1940, I read a Western American paper. It whined that England ought to be about its business, and slap down the Jap menace, walk right in and talk loud to Hitler, and altogether I think this journal would have had Great Britain fighting six simultaneous wars, while we gathered in our usual dividends. It was no use imploring the country to get

3

ready, although I had seen unbelievable striking power gathering over there beyond the Black Forest, with magnificent highways being built, all running westward.

It was no use. We became clever and blasé, quipped about the old virtues, joshed about the funny old ways, and pitied our artists and writers a little, those who wanted to be Canadian before all else. They seemed so far behind those clever Americans, realistic as the devil, cold and hard and gritty and no longer believing in Santa Claus. So far beneath the French artists. La belle Paris! La belle France! Ah! what style, what exquisite grace! And the last word, the very last! As for war? Don't be absurd! There's the British Navy; although Britain herself was rotten and bankrupt and on her last legs. And there was the invincible American Army, the greatest in the world. Won the last war you know. Marvellously ingenious people the Americans, everything the greatest in the world, though the people themselves might be a bit pushy, noisy and earthy. Between the British Navy and the American Army, and anybody else who cared to preserve the peace and look after the sanitary arrangements, we would remain in security, undisturbed in our callous grabbing and pushing. And we thought we were building a new nation, just approaching our diamond jubilee!

And so the grandchildren of those who had cleared the fields and planted, built homes and cities and defended them in all weathers, these elegant bankrupts spoke glibly about the passing of it all. They had never done an honest day's physical work in their lives; they had never sacrificed or suffered for any-

4

thing; and they squeaked that the old folks had made an awful mess of it all, and that they could be trusted to do no worse. They did nothing but talk and twitter, snitch smart tags and peppy epigrams from the bright moderns, and exhibit in public their pathetic fatigue.

Our colleges and high schools had far too many bright lads on their staffs, who had gone through on prizes and missed nothing—except life itself. They loafed in conspicuous places clad in loud tweeds and omniscience. They begged their classes to relax if, during the lectures, it seemed necessary to mention God or the Empire. It was clever to be ironical, to express elaborate pity for all those who did not share their piddling views. If the "present disorder" should collapse, they yawned, it would be too bad, too terrifically bad, but it might be borne. They never guessed that political, social and economic theories rise or fall, become sublime or puny, according to man's interpretation of his own value and dignity, his own worth; that there is more priceless theory about man and deathless fact about society in Augustine's *De Civitate Dei,* and the *Summa Theologia* of Thomas Aquinas, not to mention Calvin's *Institutes* or Wesley's *Journal,* than in half the libraries of the world on economic theory.

The teaching of history became a sort of diversion and no longer a discipline. The hard facts of history were camouflaged, compromised and diluted so as not to hurt or embarrass anyone, at home or abroad. In this appeasement of the spirit of truth, the old outlines became shadowy and the landmarks cloudy. Not believing in anything it was no longer essential to be anything, and so, bit by bit, our vocation as a people

5

all but disappeared in the chaos of our getting and spending, and trying with great determination to be gay. The teaching of literature wearied the tender pupil, and no longer became a training in taste or a disciplining of the emotions, but a form of easy reading routine, a happy diversion in the day's programme of pleasantries, all keyed down to an amorphous state called the child's own world of experience, gauged by a low vocabulary burden, by word repetition, and by the lack of anything that failed to come within the trifling range of the dull child. Literature, of course, had to disappear for want of room for reading, and the readers were given over to recreational types designed to create reading readiness, as the foreign experts called it. Even the content of the readers became more and more coloured with foreign matter, alien mental, social and political habits, until little that was fundamentally Canadian remained. Now you can't build a nation that way. When the great day of testing comes you can't raise defenders of the state fed with such spiritual puffed rice. When the need arises there will be no lusty warriors at the barricade. They will be in bed, anæmic, flimsy and effete, reading Proust and the other decadents.

II

THE ARMOURY IN OUR HALLS

A GOOD many straws in the air nowadays show us unmistakably in what direction the wind is blowing. Few doubt that the pattern of life for most of us will be drastically changed when this frightful war is over. Social, economic and political variations from current theories and styles will quite likely be startling. Tinkering in a leisurely and amiable manner with the old machinery will not do. Whatever happens, everyone will be radically affected, and everyone, young and old, will play a part — willingly or unwillingly.

1. THE WILL TO BE FREE

Just now we are chiefly concerned with the survival of Canada. For a nation at war, a sovereign state whose very existence is threatened, there is an alarming lack of basic essentials. Our foreign policy is nebulous, tentative and timid. Our national policy is vague, and anæmic. There is little understanding anywhere of our potential work and destiny. Rarely do we encounter a kindling love for our homeland; our politicians are concerned rather with election issues, boards of trade with maintaining the *status quo,* while our writers and editors are either confused or dumb. The Conference on Dominion-Provincial Relations was not scuttled by one Provincial Premier nor by three; the real saboteurs are the people of Canada numb with sleep and getting and spending.

Our first duty is to look afresh at life, the life within us as well as that without, to see it steadily and to see it whole. For too long we have summed up life as the acquirement of a group of skills, mastering a craft, a motor car or a game, conquering the weather, hard times or boredom. Amusement, news and ideas are syndicated for us; chain outlets provide us with gas, food, clothes and recreation. Only when we awake to a vivid sense of the value and dignity of life will we realize the vulgarity, absurdity and stupidity of all this. Among the titles manifold we possess, besides great men and great traditions of the past to guide us, there still remain the capacity for laughter in the presence of the ridiculous, the capacity for moral indignation and sublime anger when confronted with a great wrong, the capacity for sacrifice when the need is great.

Government, business, education, culture, the whole art of life is interpreted in terms of limits of taxation, pegged standards of living, possessions, security, power, skills. Threatened with a destroying horror we seek to recover our courage, our idealism, our souls, by forming committees on the aims of peace, the teaching of democracy and citizenship, and this after years of trying to destroy the foundations of living by our materialism and greed and hunger for power, by our weak talk of the moral bankruptcy of the Empire, and by our silly chatter about some blessed stream-lined existence outside the only working league of nations in the world sworn to defend democracy and guarantee a free citizenship—the British Empire. After having done our best to sabotage the foundations of all dignified living and the whole future of a free people, we rush madly about and hope that by organizing a committee on Democracy, by sending bulletins on Freedom to teachers and preachers, by cooking up anthologies of patriotic gems, by a whole belated series of flag-draped gestures, we can somehow hold the last barricade.

Democracy and Freedom cannot be taught out of a book. You can only believe in them, give hints of their greatness and their glory, and by dedicating a whole lifetime to them illustrate how they can be applied to every aspect of life and endeavour. This can only be done by the truly illuminated, the real rulers, the dedicated element in the nation, the winnowed minority. If ever Democracy needed an illustration of the means by which its body and soul are destroyed it can be found in the sad history of France during this generation, the callousness, perfidy, shameless materialism and cynicism among its leaders. But let us not single out humiliated France for our odium; similar signs are not lacking in Canada. Decay, unless arrested, leads inevitably to death.

2. THE WILL TO BE OURSELVES

Edward Blake, in a speech delivered at Aurora, Ontario, in 1874, declared: "The future of Canada, I believe, depends very largely upon the cultivation of a national spirit." Thomas D'Arcy McGee, in an address delivered at Montreal, a year before Confederation, stated that the literature of Canada might not be great, considered by world standards, but it was great for us, in that it was "calculated to our own meridian." Having served today well it should serve tomorrow better. The literature of a country

9

is the chief Alma Mater of the national spirit, and it should be fostered by every intelligent means. If our literature interprets accurately the Canadian social enterprise to Canadians, and if it explains Canada honestly to others, then that literature has value.

It is more essential than ever that Canada should experience a warm devotion to the arts and letters of this country. It is imperative that we should be vitally aware of them, so that they may become a living force. There is nothing so fatally easy as to become stereotyped, to ape and echo. Tradition gives way to experiment and then lapses into dead formula. Landmarks soon become hitching posts, obsessions, fads. Distrusting our own experiences and judgments, we await the oracles of London, Paris and New York, only to become mesmerized by their catchwords. Unless we can think and feel for ourselves we are doomed.

"Some citizens of a democracy have opinions that set them apart from a national effort as effectively as do lunacy, criminality or sickness." We have quite a number of folk like that. They do not think or feel, or live like Canadians, and we wonder whether they think, feel or are alive at all. It is not compulsory that one should be an author, even a Canadian author, but if one is determined to be a Canadian author one must be a Canadian author determinedly. If our writers know all that is to be known about Canada, all that needs to be known about their craft, then they might try being loyal to both for awhile—loyal and awake. Enthusiasm for one's country is no sin.

Political parties for campaign purposes have usurped the idea of national unity, and the *bonne entente,* with the result that both are greatly threatened. That is not the proper way of fostering unity. On the contrary it is highly dangerous. Our educators and writers begin to boast of their cosmopolitanism, forgetting that it is easier to be anything in the world except oneself. French and English we belong to great traditions, and we will guard by every means the literature that keeps open the highway into our own glorious past. But the French and English of Canada will see to it that their literature takes root here, shepherding east and west under its living shade.

Life is all of a piece, and we enter it when and where we must. Our racial inheritance, the soil upon which we live, our climate and basic industries, landscape and atmosphere, all qualify our way of looking at life and our manner of living it. To make any contribution of importance either to Canada or the world we must be consciously Canadian, and this national point of view will colour all our attitudes. Though we aim to view the world of letters, we see no other constructive way of doing so but through Canadian eyes and with the Canadian scene in mind.

One does not need to apologize for being oneself and standing in one's own shoes. There is no occasion for protesting that we interpret life through our own experience. If a Canadian attitude is honest it will possess value; if it is vital it will live, for a time at least or so long as there is any need for it. What is not usable in art or life is sloughed off. What does not take root and grow, reaching above the commonplace, will be ploughed under. An infinite amount of rubbish has been written about the cosmopolitan outlook, the international mind and so on. No one

11

ever shook off his inheritance, and the greatest never tried to.

As yet there is no comprehensive Canadian ideal or policy, nor any well-knit pattern of national life, and there is not likely to be until we think and act as an organism. The radio and motor car have brought us together. Opportunities for the frequent exchange of opinion multiply the number of opinions and the necessity for shouting them, but ripeness lingers beyond the microphone. We still await the fusing flame of an imperative ideal which will make of us one self-conscious people. It will come, providing we desire to be only ourselves and not somebody else. The curse of our arts and letters has been that they are monotonously derivative and imitative. We pathetically defer to foreign opinion, parrot foreign slogans, and ape foreign fashions. The strength of our French fellow citizens is due to their determination to be themselves. Tourists call them quaint. Those who know them better call them granite.

Politicians and Chambers of Commerce have told us all they know about our place and work and destiny as a people. It is all dismally inadequate. If we are to grow up, the leadership must pass to those who regard life not merely as a matter of opportunism or polite accomplishment. The life of no other country could be so rich or various as ours if we willed it to be so.

3. THE WITNESS OF HISTORY

First of all the work of Confederation must be completed. Legislators and merchants, the radio and the motor car, can never do it, but the real spokesmen and interpreters of Canada will. Confederation can not succeed if based solely upon questions of economics, industrial relations, Provincial rights, subsidies and relief. It must be founded upon spiritual and cultural values, a community of deeply felt needs, shot through with noble compassion and deep understanding. When that day arrives we shall have a nation in all reality, a true civilization. Civilization blossoms out of a living culture, and, as Spengler shows, it is that, and that alone, which determines its outward pattern as well as its life-span. One source of our weakness is, that we entrust nation building to "practical politicians," and few of those blithe realists have any adequate conception of cultural and spiritual values. Like their stable mates, the "hard-boiled business men," they are only too eager to use racial and social values and differences for their own ends. If we hand over the business of government to party whips, lobbyists and steering committees we deserve what we get, and we shall no doubt get a lot of it. These people have no recognizable policy except the will to possession and to power.

"No people without a soul can have a history." A congeries of Provinces and powers only becomes a political union when it has a common constitution, but this union still remains formless and futile until it achieves a unified living spirit, a civilization, a personality. Only out of this will evolve some day a conscious will and purpose, in other words, a destiny.

If given a chance art is art, and learning is learning, no matter where you find them, but those arts and letters that explore our native soil, explain us as a people to ourselves, and interpret us to others, to these

13

we will be especially loyal and sympathetic, for our national existence depends upon them.

"Patriotism is not enough." No, but it will help, if we stand on our own feet, speak our own idiom, and dedicate a day to good manners.

In his report to the Board of Overseers the President of Harvard University recently spoke about the teaching of the history of the United States, which has special significance for Canadians at this time.

"It is my belief that only by a deep immersion in our cultural history—the political, social, scientific and literary history of the country—can an 'education for citizenship' be achieved. But the phrase is, perhaps, deceptive. The citizens of a free democratic country are first of all independent individuals. An education which equips each man for a free and healthy emotional life would therefore seem to me to lead to the best type of citizenship. To this end we must emphasize not only mature study and discussion of the political problems of the past, but also more appreciation of the cultural forces which have shaped our history."

Among the "armoury of the invincible knights of old" was a perduring belief in the absolute rightness of their cause. Call it faith, tradition, idea, culture, destiny, or what you will, it absorbed them and made them invincible. We citizens of this young country, we Canadians, await the mobilizing of our latent idealism in order that we too may live triumphantly and invincibly.

"A Culture is born in the moment when a great soul awakens. . . . It blooms on the soil of an exactly-definable landscape, to which plant-wise it remains

14

bound. It dies when this soul has actualized the full sum of its possibilities. . . ."

Spengler eloquently traces the childhood, youth, manhood and old age through which every culture passes on its long pilgrimage from birth to death. It would be a depressing fact were we near the end of the age, the time of decline and decay, but we are not at the end; we are at the very beginning of it all. Already a new consciousness of our power and destiny awakens and stirs us. History shall yet witness a glorious culmination of the faith and idealism of this young nation in the New World.

OUR INVINCIBLE LEADERS

MANY remember the time when our universities had no place in their curriculum for Canadian History. Dr. Duncan McArthur, a recent Minister of Education for Ontario, not so long ago succeeded to the headship of the Department of History in Queen's University, that had but a few years previously established the first regular chair in Canadian History in this Dominion. Many remember the time when they asked timid questions about the existence of a Canadian Literature, and received ribald replies from the professors. Many remember when exhibitions of Canadian Art, an Art that broke with old world traditions and became definitely and consciously Canadian, evoked rowdy comment in the press. It is all as recent as that.

At last a few hardy champions here and there were joined by a growing host of acolytes, friends of Canadian arts and letters. What began as a mere whisper or twitter grew into a rolling incantation:

> We are a nation:
> We have a history;
> We have a literature;
> We have a native art!

There may be a place for incantations of this sort, but even the best incantation is no adequate substitute for deep understanding, intelligent loyalty and proud independence. Nothing important will come out of

Canada until we have the courage and the ability to know ourselves and be ourselves. As a people we are easily mesmerized by these magical formulæ, and to our own hurt. Theories and fads current abroad yesterday too often become The Thing here tomorrow. Some are innocent enough, but the disquieting fact is that we decline to grow up. Failing to think for ourselves we are consequently not sure of ourselves, and a nation not sure of itself can never keep its feet.

1. THE LEADERSHIP OF THE ÉLITE

"Government of the people, by the people, for the people"—there is possibly no better definition of Democracy. The fallacy in our thinking about Democracy, however, is that no movement is possible unless all move together. History shows us often enough that there is no truth in that. The multitude are aroused, mobilized and led by the few who can recognize truth, beauty or goodness, who can make them luminous and compelling, who can see the road that must be taken and show the way. Only the chosen people know where the Holy City may be found, and it is from them that the rest must take their definitions and their directions. Class has nothing to do with it, for the "lower" becomes the "upper" in a day. Race does not matter. The French in Canada are more Norman than Latin, and as near to the Anglo-Saxon as the Saxon is to the Celt, but what does it prove? Those who championed the ideal of chivalry, who preached the Crusades, knit Europe with its welter of races more closely than Confederation linked Canada East and West. What did matter was a fusing ideal

17

that overcame the theoretical disparities between groups.

The birth of a great nation must await a kindling flame; no nation has been born without it and none ever will. That flame first leaped to life in the breasts of a few men. This was the miracle that took place at the creation of the Russian, Italian, German and British kingdoms out of such varied materials, that created the United States, and may yet result in a really great nation here. While we call it a miracle it must be clearly understood that it was a deliberate and conscious effort, a profoundly spiritual enterprise, boldly conceived and fearlessly carried out. Historians say, that "the people were under the spell of a Culture," and that out of this grew their political style, their patterns of thought and life, their arts and letters, and their history. It is simpler, and possibly more accurate, to say that there were leaders, an élite, and that the people chose to follow them.

2. HISTORIANS AND THE PEOPLE

Truth can have little value apart from people, or the people apart from a profoundly self-conscious way of life. The conglomerate disintegrates; the crystal survives. The old learning was rich in sentiment, deep loyalties and spiritual values; today we await the oracle of the laboratory, the economist and the statistician to inform us whether they will pay their own way. This uncertainty threatens us with the exhaustion of confusion.

It is within comparatively recent years that historians of Canada have had the courage to be Canadian. The colonial point of view has largely disappeared, and with it the nostalgia for other days and other ways which plagued our arts and letters for a century. As our historians became more definitely Canadian, more certain of their own position, they ceased to patronize racial and religious groups within our borders, and they are at last beginning to put a stop to the apology, approximation and compromise which had hitherto characterized their approach to our relationship with the United States. But, given the courage to be Canadian, they have not yet written a history of the Dominion that will stir the people. Our writers can not tell a story, and the characters and events of our past offer a great challenge to the story teller and the ballad maker. The writer who can give us a history such as we need will place himself among the real leaders and makers of Canada.

Each new history of Canada tells the story with the emphasis upon the constitutional, industrial, social or political point of view, whichever happens to be in vogue at the time. There is a nice balance of space between the French Régime and the British Régime, between the East and West, but there is no corresponding balance between what is supremely important and what is mere filler, between what will flatter this group and what will set goals for all our striving. There is little justification for constitutional history at all in our schools, certainly not until the story of Canada has first been learned by *heart*. Research students have mined a vast hoard of new gold for the writers of school histories, and this story must be told in the elementary grades, in the intermediate grades, until our boys and girls are thrilled by it. We hear complaints everywhere that Canadians are too casual, too indifferent even at a time when our nation, our Empire, the very edifice of our lives, are threatened with extinction. But how can we honestly expect the people to be proud, strong, alive and united, if the story of their country is rarely or never presented to them in such a way as to suggest that they should be? No one lives or dies for a thing he does not understand, believe in, love, feel a part of himself.

So we await leaders in the field of history who can pick their way among the fluctuating theories, among educational methods founded upon the practice of England, Scotland, France, Germany and the United States, and among the wholesale importations of curricular carpentry and content, and remain uncompromisingly Canadian. Pupils in the lower grades are guided through the simple social experiences of the home school and neighbourhood, and this is all to the good. But from there on, during the most impressionable years of the pupils' lives, they are taken by train, airplane, ship and submarine round the world—see every country but their own. In only three grades out of thirteen do they read Canadian history, and that too often is very badly written. In a country so sprawling, vast and conglomerate as this Dominion can we build on that? Will Confederation succeed without some vital integrating core, a kindling, fusing passion and ideal? We think not. The recommendations of the Rowell-Sirois Report have to do with economic problems, with relief, social welfare, and ultimately with the constitution, and we shall yet have to consider that Report, but the success of its application must wait upon the revitalizing and integration of the nation's soul. Before we are in a position to make history, we shall have to tarry until we have those who can write the story of Canada in such a compelling way as will lift us out of our lethargy and point the road forward.

3. LITERATURE AND LIFE

Good poetry and prose are of great practical value to a people. They preserve the purity of the nation's idiom, keep alive valuable ideas, offer an indispensable discipline of the emotions, and inspire standards of taste, but most of all they represent a certain type of experience. A nation's literature and a nation's life have many things in common, chief of which is the common soil of time and place and need. When a nation's literature is at a low ebb, numb and demoralized, the nation's life is flat, uninspired and confused. It would be a venture of the highest importance if a national ministry of culture were established for the express purpose of assisting and encouraging the arts and letters of Canada. Meanwhile, and at a time when we face the greatest challenge in our history, our writers are either dumb or insignificant.

Apologists for Canadian letters offer various alibis for our present state of ineptitude. The times are not auspicious; materialism has leaped to the saddle and rides mankind. There is no market at home, and little pay. Business, even the management of great daily papers, can scarcely be persuaded that books have any practical value in the scheme of things, and writers and critics must be tolerated at the best, or made to pay their way at the worst. And they insist that there is no sympathetic and understanding atmosphere in which a creative writer can hope to do any work. There is no doubt some truth in all this, but one questions whether Chaucer, Shakespeare or Dostoevsky found conditions more congenial or propitious.

What we are concerned with here is not the pampering of our poets, but in making sure we have a few worthy the name, and that we understand and value them for what they are worth. At the very best there can be but one or two of the unquestioned élite, and those that follow them will be few in numbers. Yet, when the whole story of a people is told, the crowning glory of its civilization and its gift to the ages unborn will be its writers and artists.

If there is any truth in this, every care should be taken to keep these gifted representatives of our culture near the centre of our national life, and make sure that the coming generations of Canadians do not forget the accents of their noble speech.

The easiest way out for educationists is to hand the business of teaching literature over to the precisionists and pedants. It is all simplified into a matter of measurements, vocabulary burden, word recognition, frequency of repetition, first level types and second level types and activity types and so on. Readers for the grades, uncounted hosts of them, are scribbled by ambitious teachers for ambitious publishers on ambitious theories. Readers in literature and readers in the social studies are almost interchangeable. Fine prose is rewritten; poetry is altered and edited; taste and the sense of style are ironed out of them, and all to bring the readers within the reach of the mediocre child, and of those with an impoverished vocabulary. The result is not literature; it is not even education.

Great poetry and prose—through diction, cadences, metaphors and ideas—evoke more than mere magic, more than bare meanings. William James used to say that words have fringes, something beyond themselves, hints and suggestions of beauty and truth that require trained intelligence, alert sensibility and disciplined emotions to follow them, understand them and relish them. Literature is an experience, the exalted experience of a great writer, the distilled experience of a nation, and we are in danger of destroying the ability to understand and appreciate great literature. The literature of a nation is its very life, and we should turn to it as our chief mentor. We must choose the best and build up to that, not water down the content to match the jaded interests and tastes of today's children. Children do not know what they want, and whatever they want it will not be for long. The fad for variety, the departure from literature that has stood the test, is largely a publishers' frolic and young ambition's ladder. All this will pass.

Literature tells us what life is, and how we may cope with it. Through literature we become tinglingly aware not only of life as a spectacle but of life as a rich and deathless experience. Word recognition is all to the good, but words are often mountains high and oceans deep, even short easy-looking words. It is not a matter of syllables, but their proud traditions and exalted meanings, their flavour and texture, contour and colour, that no pedant will ever guess.

Is it not true, that for ninety-five out of a hundred the course in literature will be the chief and perhaps the only training they will receive in taste, the only discipline of the emotions they will ever know, the only opportunity to grow ripe and poised and sure of themselves? No reading skill will ever compensate for the loss of this. No second-hand retelling of great prose and verse by third-rate editors will ever do. It is all too shoddy. You can not divorce style from literature; it is more than personality, more than technique; it is the very body of art. Therefore this craze for simplicity will prove a costly experiment.

The cosmopolite has no history because he has no strong, undivided ego, no well-defined home, no pure native language, no lofty sense of duty or destiny. The voices of the world's great centres may be urbane, bland, sophisticated, but there is no high purpose in them, and no nation can survive without that. No nation can achieve its true destiny that adopts without profound and courageous reasoning and selection the thought and styles of another, that prefers the arts and letters of a foreign state to its own, that would rather be anything else under the stars than its own true self. If we hope to be a nation our people and their arts and institutions must take root in this soil. If we expect to retain our place in the British Commonwealth, then our roots must go down deep into that living stream of tradition. There are the sources of our life and power, and dearly must we prize them.

Our invincible leaders and greatest legislators are our historians, our creative writers, our poets and our artists. We depend upon them to awaken our nation, to quicken all our life. They are the responsible minority, clearest of eye, strongest of heart, and with them stand a few teachers and interpreters, who have "the power to hold the others spellbound by a power derived from what they have experienced." The days ahead will be dark indeed for all of us unless we can have this leadership of our true élite.

"So long as a people is a nation, and works out the Destiny of a nation, there is in it a minority which in the name of all represents and fulfils its history."

4. FREE MEN IN A FREE DEMOCRACY

In the Summer of 1944, and at precisely the right moment for such a manifesto, there appeared a small brochure entitled *Literature in American Education*. It bore the explanatory sub-heading: "An Important Timely Statement prepared for the Modern Language Association of America by a Special Committee of its Commission on Trends in Education." The Enoch Pratt Free Library of Baltimore reprinted this document in a very attractive format, and at a price equivalent to a gift. With their permission we quote the following extracts:

I

Shall we deprive ourselves of our inheritance? The writers of this report are concerned for that inheritance. Ours is a plea for the validity of literary studies in American Education. . . . To doubt that literature should have a high place in the education of mankind is to apologize for the very nature of man himself. He has always turned towards drama, poetry, fiction, and many forms of prose as sources of instruction, inspiration, or delight. He will continue to do so in the years to come. . . . In modern thought on education there exists a surprising misconception of the place of literary studies. If these inadequate ideas prevail, our American students will be severely impoverished. They will miss something important to

25

themselves, something even more important to the democratic society of which they are a part.

II

The hobby-lobby curriculum: The situation that threatens us just now is due to competition. The curricula of our schools and colleges have been made a kind of "hobby-lobby." Every impulse is now a "subject", and we bestow academic credit upon mental activities once regarded as merely pleasant forms of conversation. We have concocted an endless Christmas morning in which both teachers and pupils rush from one bright novelty to another beneath the shining educational tree. . . . Gradually there has arisen the widely held tenet, that literary studies, once a central part of education, may now be regarded as the luxurious appendages of man's training in a scientific, political world. Germany has said so—Germany from which so much of our culture came. It is suspected, moreover, that humane letters are merely the remnant of an out-moded "aristocratic" education, in which they were often diverted from their true meaning to become the badge of snobs, the toy of the rich and idle. . . .

III

Literature, servant of both the individual and society. Letters, in the opinion of some present-day educationists, should be wholly or chiefly contemporary letters, books linked easily with "life" and our practical up-and-coming world. . . . Among the most profound justifications ever made for literary studies is the answer Matthew Arnold gave at Cambridge, in 1882, to Huxley's contention, that literature should yield to science its high place in general education, inasmuch as science offers that up-to-date and practical knowledge which should form the staple instruction of all men. . . . Science, he argues, will never ultimately take the place of humane letters because the constitution of human nature will never allow this change. . . . Arnold sees the work of literature as a truly social work. . . . It does not try to teach down to the level of inferior classes; it does not try to win them for this or that sect of its own, with ready-made judgments and watchwords. It seeks the harmonious good of all men by administering to all the powers that make up men's lives. . . .

All the modern apologist for literary studies has to do is follow the ramifications of that argument—to show how, even in our scientific and socially conscious world, letters do call out men's lives at more points; how they truly motivate and correlate all his other studies and interests; how they place the many parts of his life in harmony and relationship and thus give him, in the exact sense of the word, integrity; how they train him for responsible citizenship in a democratic American society.

Our education needs, therefore, to create men and women who have received from the past and from the present, both from their own country and from foreign lands, a true enlargement of mind and emotion; who have had more than fleeting glimpses of that beauty and truth and goodness which is as much man's claim upon the world as is his claim for food and water, air and sun; who have known sympathy, compassion, and toleration.

The total effect is that literature is certainly not regarded as an embroidery upon life but as a revelation of life itself. The student no longer thinks of it as something about a lark, a nightingale, and a lover, interesting as all three of these may be. He sees it as any significant expression of the human situation. He sees it as the study that can correlate all his other studies; for the very life of literature is this power of correlation. . . . For experience in literature helps us, not merely to find our way among the intricacies of social and business life, but also to enter so completely into the thoughts and feelings of others that our perception and understanding contribute powerfully to the unity of civilization. . . . For literature, like life, in time consumes its own freaks and desperadoes, setting finally in clearer light than ever

> One great society alone on earth:
> The noble Living and the noble Dead.

IV

· *Increased experience in quality:* Widely viewing the different images of life in books, man suspects that all things are not of equal worth. He builds and refines his own system of values through the process of experiencing a multitude of choices vicariously—choices that his normal life, his so-called "practical" life, would not afford him. The student of letters becomes aware, both with his mind and with his emotions, of the laws that govern mankind. . . . The experience in quality afforded by humane letters arises, moreover, from much besides their contents. It comes also with the effect of their style. *For life has accent as well as substance. . . . Style has, furthermore, a way of exposing what is false; for when little things aspire to be said in a big way, their littleness is clearly revealed.* Style can establish preferences in the blood and silently influence the choices of a lifetime. . . .

V

For man must return at last upon himself. After society has done its best for him in the political and economic sphere, it leaves him finally in his own company. The highest function of a democracy being to insure the sacred rights of personality, the final act of such a government is to restore man to himself—to give him back the privacy that is rightly his. In practice this return is made anyhow, under freedom or under slavery. You educate man for the society in which he lives; but *you educate him ultimately for this inevitable solitude, for those authoritative hours in which he discovers his own depth.* Reflecting on the ways of life and death, conscious of mortal hopes and fears, a man then decides what he is. Here is the last test of his education. In such moments he is not the economic man, the political man, or even the man of science. The help of science will be limited, because its changing facts will continue to be discovered after he is dead. In a sense, he cannot wait for science. The affinities he must detect, the loyalties he must now declare, must arise from another source. They must come from out the whole life of man, the "man of flesh and bone"; from out the estimate placed on him by those who have thought and felt most deeply and have best expressed their thought and feeling. If he cannot draw on the humane past and receive help from those who have lived before him, he will have the limited vision of one who must judge the quality of things without true perspective. And he will be confused and alone when he might have been part of a great confederation. A whole dimension will have been taken from him.

VI

Human liberty depends not on charters and institutions alone. It depends on memory and the ancient heritage of men, on the voice of that humane confederation, scattered through many lands and through many ages, which it is the business of literature to make known. We have been progressively forgetting that heritage and trying to live as children without parents or teachers to guide them. In a recent statement of his faith in liberal education, Mr. Wendell Willkie, in an issue of *The American Scholar,* puts the challenge squarely before us: "When you range back and forth through the centuries, when you weigh the utterance of some great thinker or absorb the meaning of some great composition, in painting or music or poetry; when you live these things within yourself and measure yourself against them—only then do you become an initiate in the world of the free." This is the true freedom we covet for our children here.

29

REHEARSAL FOR SUICIDE

CONFEDERATION was devised by man, and by man it can be destroyed. The mistakes we have made, both English and French, have been countless. We have frequently put it all down to our adolescence, but the fault is our stupidity and deliberate perverseness. We are wilfully wrong-headed.

1. RITUAL FOR DEATH

Before the war many of our fatigued intellectuals informed us that the empire was morally bankrupt and was on the way out. They assured us that Confederation was definitely going to collapse. The reason was not that Canada and the Empire had fulfilled their divine destiny and were to be scrapped, but that a lot of anæmic patriots were either too frail to fight for them or in some perverse way desired to see them fall.

The Canadian people, at one time or another, have experimented with practically every known type of national suicide. In the early days it was colonialism, the paralyzing deference to the parent state, that suffocated and sterilized every enterprise best suited for our natural development. This has been dying a hard death, and may still be seen in the insularity, provincialism and antipathy to change in many parts of the country.

There are those who have seen in Puritanism a particularly unbeautiful form of self-destruction. It is supposed to be a symbol for everything that is negative, repressive, dull and strangling. It is said to kill the arts, deaden letters, and suck all the joy out of life. But Canada has not been unique in this, and, as in every land, non-conformity is balanced somewhere by conformity, protest by assent, puritanism by catholicism, tears by laughter. At the moment it does not appear any too obvious that Puritanism is likely to destroy us by its austere disciplines. There are puritans and latitudinarians in every church, society and family. They will likely cancel out each other rather than kill us.

The form of suicide we have most to fear is the wilful negation of all belief, all religion, and all sense of direction of any sort. There are many, no doubt, who were not Nazis, yet they did nothing against the growing menace. Infamy and depravity, plunder and slavery, poisonous ideology and insolent abuse of power, these went unchallenged in any effective way. Once there might have been time, but when brutishness took firm command, and the world was in torment, it was too late. Germany and the world together paid for their sins and sped headlong toward the abyss.

The surest kind of suicide, for it has never been known to fail, is unbelief. Earlier in this book there was offered a catalog of our blind unbeliefs as a nation, and each one of them has been a tentative experiment in self-destruction. We list them again before we pass on to a few special and more spectacular brands of suicide.

(i) As a people we have no national sense of direction, of vocation, or destiny. The result is that we are easily lost in a fumbling, groping, quicksand and bog of expediency.

(ii) Failing to read the lessons of our own past, and blind to the real nature of our destiny, we inhabit a twilight world, a place of noisy confusion, deprived of guiding light or even a symbol, not even so much as a banner, a hymn, or any universally agreed upon countersign or emblem of a joint devotion and dedication.

(iii) We have made no inventory of our physical wealth, although we have bragged most often about our unlimited resources. Therefore, we continue to squander and despoil it, and guarantee that those who come after us will subsist upon a mined out land. If the soil is a symbol of the kind of people who dwell upon it, then we are going to have a thin, scrawny, hard-bitten and derelict race. Our shiftlessness is cosmic; it extends to everything. There is a sleep so profound as to be akin to death.

(iv) A young nation requires nothing so much as the simple desire to be only itself. Yet from the beginning we have been plagued by an itch for cosmopolitanism. Few were aware that there is scarcely anything so sterilizing or enervating as that bland disease.

(v) Growing out of this specially weak and silly mimicry of others, with its hang-dog attitude toward itself, there persisted for decades the most callous indifference to our native arts, letters and crafts. We still have no national library. Many of our Provincial Archives are but names. Few art galleries are supported in any sustained or generous way. We still have no chair of Canadian Literature in any college. There is no federal portfolio for culture that might stimulate and diffuse our birthright arts and letters, let alone hold any kind of a lamp up to learning.

32

Writers and artists work with little acknowledgment, and often are on the brink of penury, yet neither this rich Dominion nor any Province provides any pension, or budgets for any grants in aid, for those who have made the name of Canada to shine but now are in grievous need. Surely this has been rehearsing for suicide in desperate earnest.

(vi) It was pointed out that the dance masters at this saraband of death were the élite. We shall not repeat here the hard things we said about them, the shocking treason of our educators. They too were wilful, as wilful as weak. No strong, proud people could ever in this world emerge out of teaching like that. It was tainted with death because there was no life in it. Was there ever a people who aspired to selfhood, who were made to look so petty by their historians, critics and biographers, pygmies against the back-drop of this northern empire?

And what we have said about education in particular may be expanded to include education in general. It brings us back again to our fatal lack of a sense of direction, of vocation. Because of that we fiddle and fumble, and inch nearer and nearer the brink of the abyss.

Mr. Walter Lippman has remarked, that, "deprived of their cultural tradition, the newly educated western men no longer possess in the form and substance of their own minds and spirits, the ideas, the premises, the rationale, the logic, the method, the values, or the deposited wisdom which are the genius of the development of western civilization. The prevailing education is destined, if it continues, to destroy western civilization, and is in fact destroying it."

2. A Shroud for Culture

In 1882 Ernest Renan asked the question: "Qu'est ce qu'une Nation?" He provided his own answer, and it was in part this: "Une nation est une âme, un principe spirituel. Deux choses qui, a vrai dire, ne font qu'une, constituent cette âme, ce principe spirituel. L'une est dans le passé, l'autre dans le présent. L'une est la possession d'une riche legs de souvenirs, l'autre le consentement actuel, le désir de vivre ensemble, la volonté de faire valoir l'héritage qu'on a reçu indivis."

French Canada has stressed this to the exclusion of many things. Culture is a spiritual principal. Nourished by the past, it grows rich in its legacies and symbols. It tends to become an exclusive possession, even a barrier.

This is not the place to attempt an analysis of either French or English culture. It is enough for the present purpose to point out that the back bone of France, as of Quebec, is the farmer. He is a sturdy, independent, thrifty and stubborn type. He can be gay among known friends and allies, and most charming when nothing important is at stake. He loves his own hearth, and distrusts outsiders on principle. Home-loving, home-staying, he is self-sufficient, indifferent to the world or its opinions. The great revolutions, social and political and industrial, have largely passed him by. He is neither an empire man nor a national man; he is a parish man and above all a family and home man. The currents of the world's thought and life do not bother him. He is not naturally excited about Protestants or hysterical about Jews. He will help anyone gladly and not look for gratuities, neither will he refuse honest pay for honest work. He looks up to no one better than himself or down upon any one he feels inferior. Proud of his own strength and no man's fool, he stands up at times against his curé but never against religion. "We remain," says André Siegfried, "the republic of little people . . . preoccupied with 'the continuous struggle of the small against the great.' "

Old France tended to dissolve in dilettantism, always arriving at truth but never getting there. Art and life broke up into a vast and varied congeries of schools and parties. New France grew gradually more dogmatic, and its dogmatism tended to reach its apotheosis in a Myth. Old France prided herself on her logic, her dialectics, her clarity and genius for style. New France had little pride at all, but aimed in its blunt Norman way to work out a usable philosophy of life, and in short this was a stubborn defiance of anything that insulted the soul.

We shall return in a moment to this business of symbol and myth. For the present it is only necessary to say, that while Old France faded away in symbolism and the précieuse, in dilettantism and the spirituelle gone mad, New France turned from all such and agreed with Voltaire, "Il faut cultiver notre jardin."

There is always danger ahead for any Chosen People. By their very sense of vocation, of difference, they are apt to retreat further and further into the Promised Land of the spirit and permit the world to pass them by. The fertilizing events of history have left too slight a deposit in Quebec. Such a sheltered people are too open to the organized treason of the Rulers. They grow increasingly bewildered listening to the conflicting party cries. Survival must come through a greater participation in the work of the whole nation, and not in escape. Jean Baptiste does not yet regard himself as one with all Canada. He still thinks in terms of colonization and parishes and not in terms of Canada as a whole. He is schooled in the duty of participating in Peace River and other French Canadian empire movements, and constantly encouraged to be mindful of his rights, his share in government jobs, and all else, but the time has surely come to dwell a little more upon obligations and duties respecting his homeland as a whole and not merely *la patrie,* Laurentie.

Culture may be a shroud. The culture of a group, that cuts it off from the living culture of the world about, is merely an escape from reality. Culture that mistrusts the practical and utilitarian, the scientific and coldly efficient, may be quaint and lovable, but it will not be impressive or long-lived. This sort of culture escapes into folk-lore and away from the reality of the broad living world. There is no future for that. Where the English are threatened with death because of their lack of both symbol and political dogma, the French are in equal danger because they have made of dogma and symbol an ivory tower. There is a happy medium. We must yet find it, and we must find it together.

3. The Battle of Slogans

Despots and slave runners contended merely for the bodies of men and women, today they cry, "It is your souls we want." The art of vassalage has been refined to a diabolical point of efficiency. In many nations it begins with the cradle and is unremitting through all the grades of school. Political action, sectarianism, social welfare, industrial organization, wherever you look there is a noose dangling above the heads of the unsuspecting. "Nations do not love each other," remarked Joseph de Maistre. Well, neither do people as a rule. The human heart is capable of loving but few; it does very well to like the many. Perhaps the best we can aim at is general respect and good will.

There seems, however, to be loose in the world, and especially in this world of Canada, a particularly malignant devil. The more one studies this the more certain one becomes that it is the very incarnation of evil. You can not nail this satanic thing down, or corner him as any one man or group. You can only follow him about by the diabolical and lying slogans he leaves everywhere.

What misshapen mind first invented the colossal heresy of isolation, "l'achat chez nous"? Who first dreamed that a people must never forget its past, never forget an injury or humiliation, or ever suffer change? Who first said, "Mon Maitre, le Passé"? If cunning wickedness ever devised a sword to destroy itself it was the scoundrel who first spoke of "la revanche des berceaux." "The revenge of the cradles!" That is a war cry. It is quite the thing to speak of "les maudits anglaises," but the English, are they so incurably stupid? After all that is a harmless kind of banter, recalling the English speaking Canadian's jokes about French Canadian families, and on a par with the Pat and Mike yarn or the Scotch gag. But these others are threats and battlecries. Do not the perpetrators realize that? Out upon them!

The English Canadian has much to answer for in his treatment of the French, particularly his unblushing manipulation of the prejudices of these decent, simple folk for unholy political purposes. Nothing the French may say or do can ever equal the hideous wrong we have done him in jockeying him for his vote. We have encouraged his isolation, heaped up the fires of his prejudices, strengthened his fears, exploited him, herded him, and now we curse him because he can't unlearn it all in a minute before we all go over the abyss.

The French leaders, however, have still some way to go before we can ever hope to build a nation together in good will. The first task is the rewriting of the history of Canada. In no Province is history so mutilated, so designed to foster prejudice, as in Quebec. What may one hope for from a serious manual that glosses over the ghastly and epic years 1940-1944, and merely records that the great event was the founding of the Oratory of Brother André? What can you say for history like this: "Le peuple canadien-francais constitue une nation." "La race canadienne-francaise est de race pure, exempte de tout métissage." "L'Americanisme entre chez nous non pas comme un voleur, mais comme un gangster." Those are legends designed for the walls of schools in Quebec.

Further on the French Canadian is taught that he has had no training in democracy, that it is not native to him, and requires time to perfect. But the French lived through the time of the revolutions in England, France and the United States. There have always been republicans and republican movements in Quebec. If the core of Democracy means the majority will of all the people, are the leaders of Quebec making that clear? Or is democracy a matter of convenience, like national unity? You will do nothing to threaten unity if we dislike it. Heads I win, tails you lose. No, it can't possibly be that.

The French are also told that they have had no training in war. The very foundation of New France was with the sword in one hand and an implement in the other. Under the seigneurs they were conscripted for military service, for there was no other way to protect the young colony but by equal service and sacrifice. They knew then that there could be no half-wars; that war was all or nothing, life or death. There never was such a thing as a moderate war. Who invented those heresies? Who sold them to these honest, lovable people? War work for high wages is not war. It is luxury. And if the nation goes on strict gas and food rations, it is not clever to evade the regulations wholesale. Who taught the honest peasants that it was the right thing to do? Were they the same scoundrels who urged them to ignore the call to arms? Who boasted, one political group in rising crescendo above the other, that the countryside was as full of young men as ever, when whole communities of English Canadians were stripped of their boys? Are they the same rogues who took over from Lenin, their arch heretic, the lie that this was an imperialist war? Are they the same wolves who repeated, until it became gospel truth, that Quebec was a state within the state, self-determining, and that they would march to defend it when it was attacked? The British North America Act, and Confederation, let alone Democracy, are they cloaks to shelter self interest only?

There is nothing like this in English speaking Canada. It is so vicious as to be unreal. We have many brands of wickedness but we never sent our children to school to hate.

"Our history is not written as it should be for those who believe that harmony between the two great races living in this country is possible and desirable," said Senator Bouchard. "I have given typical examples of how our Canadian history is taught in Quebec. They clearly demonstrate this teaching cannot be according to the facts and that it is made intentionally to prejudice the young minds against our compatriots of a different tongue and creed. It is un-Canadian and un-Christian. The Founder of Christianity has never tried to raise one man against another because of difference in race and language." (Senator Bouchard)

That way lies death! No people can indefinitely stand that sort of thing. It atrophies the soul of a people, cankers it and destroys it. Out of that comes something dwarfed and cruelly misshapen. The world has no use for people who study to misunderstand and hate like that. The world by-passes them, goes round them and goes away and leaves them to wither and die.

Yet that is not the attitude of all the people. There still remains the gallant and honest world of the Golden Age of French Canada, and many are the élite who believe in it and follow it. This is how Garneau spoke of his beloved people in the fifth edition of his *Histoire du Canada:*

"Les Canadiens-Français forment un peuple de cultivateurs, dans un climat rude et sévère. Ils n'ont pas, en cette qualité, les manières élégantes et fastueuses des populations méridionales; mais ils ont de la

40

gravité, du caractère et de la persévérance. Ils en ont donné des preuves depuis qu'ils sont en Amérique, et nous sommes convaincu que ceux qui liront leur histoire de bonne foi, reconnaîtront qu'ils se sont montrés dignes des deux grandes nations aux destinées desquelles leur sort s'est trouvé ou se trouve encore lié.

"Ils n'auraient pu être autrement sans démentir leur origine. Normands, Bretons, Tourangeaux, Poitevins, ils descendent de cette forte race qui marchait à la suite de Guillaume le Conquérant, et dont l'esprit, enraciné ensuite en Engleterre, a fait des habitants de cette petite île une des premières nations du monde; ils viennent de cette France qui se tient à la tête de la civilisation européenne depuis la chute de l'empire romain, et qui, dans la bonne comme dans la mauvaise fortune, se fait toujours respecter; de cette France qui, sous ses Charlemagne comme sous ses Napoléon, ose appeler toutes les nations coalisées à des combats de géants; ils sont sortis surtout de cette Vendée normande, bretonne, angevine, dont le monde admire le dévouement sans bornes pour les objets de ses sympathies, et dont l'admirable courage acouvert de gloire le drapeau qu'elle leva au milieu de la Révolution française.

"Que les Canadiens soient fidèles à eux-mêmes; qu'ils soient sages et persévérants, qu'ils ne se laissent point séduire par le brillant des nouveautés sociales et politiques! Ils ne sont pas assez forts pour se donner carrière sur ce point. C'est aux grands peuples à faire l'épreuve des nouvelles théories: ils peuvent se donner toute liberté dans leurs orbites spacieuses. Pour nous, une partie de notre force vient de nos traditions; ne nous en éloignons ou ne les changeons que graduellement. Nous trouverons dans l'histoire de notre métropole elle-même de bons examples à suivre. Si l'Angleterre est grande aujourd'hui, elle a eu de terribles tempêtes à essuyer, la conquête étrangère à maîtriser, des guerres religieuses à éteindre et bien d'autres traverses. Sans vouloir prétendre à si haute destinée, notre sagesse et notre ferme union adouciront beaucoup nos difficultés, et, en excitant leur intérêt, rendront notre cause plus sainte aux yeux des nations."

Sometimes one wonders whether it would not be better to close up the subsidized social agencies, and even give parliament and the church a holiday, trusting to the native decency of men for awhile. Such dreadful deeds are committed in the name of government and organized religion. Men must continue to fight and die together in millions because their spiritual leaders refuse to kneel and pray together.

The plain folk are the real custodians of the national morality. Eloquent organizers of labour, rhetorical friends of the people, unctuous champions of free enterprise, push forward in all directions in a tidal wave of vast good will, that each succeeding wave cancels out. It is, as Alfred Noyes points out, something more than a political or economic conflict; it is in reality a "battle for the possession of the human soul."

"How can we build a stable world again . . . when the very foundations of all real belief have been shattered or sneered out of existence, in the intellectual and spiritual collapse of Western civilization? . . . For more than half a century, in the literature of the pseudo-intellectuals and neo-pagans all over the world, the sapping and mining has been carried on, with a curiously malicious ardour or concentration, confusing all the lines of right and wrong, and all the loyalties of mankind." (*The Edge of the Abyss*)

4. THE CULT OF FEAR

Fear is the Father of Hate. In spite of the fact that religious and political leaders in all parts of the country expostulate against hatred, there are others, the very dregs of their profession, who thrive upon mischief and never weary of sowing suspicion and waving the torch of fear. At election times we have witnessed some tragic exhibitions of this. Apparently our leaders will never grow up.

Of late, relationships between the French and English have gone from bad to worse. Much of it can be traced to the wilful malice of a few men, to the hunger for power of a few men, to the prostitution of the priestly function by a few fanatics. If the French had all these imbeciles we could be magnanimous and pity them, but we have our full share and we hang our heads.

On their side the French fear that their 30 per cent. will be swamped in the nation, and that the majority will coerce them into war, into economic slavery and so on. In retaliation they confuse matters by bundling all English speaking persons together as Protestants, thereby kindling the indignation of a large number of Roman Catholics as loyal to their Church as any French Canadian. The French leaders never made any political blunder equal to this silly branding of English as the idiom of the heretic. No one can remedy this but the leaders of the French themselves.

The French have also raised another bogey that is

43

dangerous in the extreme. They speak of their race, and its proper destiny. They reason that the race has its dignities and must not be controlled by foreigners, meaning the English. To live and die for *notre belle province* is the duty of a loyal heart. This, then, is their own preserve, and others are outsiders. But the English know very well that this same reasoning applies to the Maritimes, parts of Ontario, Manitoba and Alberta, and that in Provinces thought their own, the English are squeezed out of whole counties and once more called *étrangers*. Where will it end?

Language is more than a convenient idiom. French, we are told, is the vehicle by which the greatest splendours of religion have been celebrated. It is the language of the most glorious company of men and women who have carried the cross to the infidel. Stated like that language becomes something quite different, indeed something explosive. Language can be either a covered bridge between peoples, or it can become a wall of spears driving them apart.

Now the English have enough to repent of, but never have they spoken that way. No English speaking person ever thinks of his language as the true vehicle of Protestantism or anything else. He never thinks of himself, except it be at some extremist club that is paltry in numbers and power, as having a racial or British mission. But he does back up with surprise when his compatriots go on to say, that the English scoured the prisons for recruits as immigrants, sifted poorhouses, and swept the streets for men to send out and overwhelm the French in Canada. So the apostles of a pure race urge vigilance against these sweepings, "les vagabonds," "les parasites de l'émigration." Thus is the cult of fear recruited in a fantastic way by the scum of the earth, the venal confessors and tribunes of the French people. Either they know this invites civil war or they are blind and stupid.

"The cultivation of prejudices is like that of microbes. Both grow fast and both are dangerous. We shall not undertake to examine the consciences of certain of our English-speaking compatriots. That delicate task we leave to our English-speaking friends. Let us turn rather to our own task. Let us root out amongst ourselves whatever obstacles to good understanding between the two Canadian groups may be found . . . Certain of these obstacles are to be found in our treatment of history, especially in the history books which we place in the hands of our youth. When used by prejudiced teachers such textbooks instil hatred slowly but surely . . . Get away from prejudice and you will banish hatred, and fear, too, though that may prove a more difficult task. Garneau writes: 'They (the French Canadian people) are bound up in themselves'; and again, 'Their entire political policy may be summed up as self-preservation. . . .' You cannot believe that Garneau writes like one disillusioned. He cannot be accused of either defeatism or pessimism. But it may be said that Garneau did not dare to go beyond the situation which circumstances had created for us. . . . To preserve themselves just as they were, that was the objective which Garneau assigned to the French Canadian people. This meant making tradition, even prejudice, and the imitation of others, the masters of our destiny." (Abbé Arthur Maheux)

Again we ask, who is responsible for this wicked

poisoning of the people? Can they not be hunted out and hanged?

French speaking Canadians have urged that English Canadians should understand their interests and needs. There is a genuine wish in English speaking Canada to do that very thing. As a matter of fact, English speaking Canadians have made pilgrimages to Quebec for pleasure or for study in an unbroken stream for generations. Artists have always sought out Quebec as a very haven of delight. Our writers have described the French and their Province in a library of books. Many French Canadian works have been translated into English. Very few English works have been translated into French. A good many subscribe to French papers in English speaking Canada, but there are relatively very few French subscribers to English periodicals. In fact there are large numbers of English Canadians who speak and write about French Canada with genuine good will and even affection, and have been doing so for years, but only of late years have a few French Canadians come forward to take their place in this growing community of better understanding.

There are things we both can meet and conquer. The fiddling politician who builds up his brief day upon nasty appeals to secessionists and isolationists, to racialists and anti-war fanatics, this kind of pigmy can be handled. The blustering vote-snatcher who rants about imperialistic wars, and who hopes to keep a solid Grit or Tory bloc even if it means secession from the British Commonwealth of Nations, he can be roared down. The guileless fellow who cackles about the quaintness of Quebec, who lisps that *les habitants*

46

are virtuous and simple and unlearned in the intricacies of democracy or world affairs, this lad can be pushed aside. These men have sung to the one tune so long that it has ceased either to instruct or entertain. Like so much of the literature of French Canada, it repeats the same thing too often, as if done to a formula. All this is obvious, simple and out in the light.

The thing we fear is Fear itself. It is the venomous little underground cabal that will never let the people forget the Acadian expulsion, or any other English slight or wrong in all their history. The humiliations of the French Court were frequent and real, the plunder of the King's agents unscrupulous. The repair of a Quebec belfry had to be referred to Colbert. The King declined the repeated requests of the colony for a printing press. The French in Canada never regarded France as a real motherland as the Irish or Scotch do. They had been plundered, dragooned and then abandoned, and good riddance. Forsaken and alone, there was born this race and religion awfulness. It has increased until it has become the very apotheosis of prejudice and racial hatred. It has evolved into a kind of Islam, and its Koran is *Maria Chapdelaine* and the extremist writings of fanatical priests and journalists. Here is the bible of all the prejudices, the very gospel of hysterical hatred. It is stated with passion, and often with a wild kind of beauty; occasionally it attains distinction of style, but at root, and in all its forms, it is an evil and corrupt thing.

This new Islam in Canada is something to despise and dread. There is nothing like it in any other Province, and indeed in few nations, young or old. It has created unholy fear. Revenge of the cradles can only mean a new kind of racial and religious imperialism. The passionate return to the past can only mean the triumph of a mediæval state which will turn Canada back among the third rate powers, back with Spain, Mexico and the rest. The exultant proclamation of race-religion, of a French and Catholic state, can only mean civil war. That nonsense belongs to the old world, and to a past wicked age. We will have none of it. If there are any Protestant wild men itching for a religious war may they perish. If there are any English spellbinders fooling around with warmed up memories of the Boyne and St. Bartholomew's may they too perish miserably.

Where are the men of good will in Canada, French and English? Will they now come forward and form themselves into a Canadian Legion of Honour. Are there a dozen such in both languages, who will swear fidelity each to the other, vow to guard the interests and needs of the other, come war or peace, come hell or high water? If such there be, they shall save the state, even though they be so few, so very few.

5. GOVERNMENT BY BLACKMAIL

In their best moments the pioneers from France and Britain, as well as their descendants—the fathers of Confederation and the builders of our democracy— have had a profound sense of duty and destiny. In these enlightened moments they might well have echoed the words of John Ruskin:

"When we build, let us think that we build forever. Let it not be for the present delight nor for present

48

use alone. Let it be such work as our descendants will thank us for; and let us think as we lay stone on stone, that a time is to come when these stones will be held sacred."

In their worst moments the ethnic groups of which we are composed have proceeded upon the assumption, that rights were secured and advancement made by a species of blackmail. In a country where national honours and federal cabinet appointments are allotted not only on geographical lines, but on racial and religious lines as well, you have the ideal set-up for government by blackmail. As a matter of fact union government in Canada began with a series of mysterious gestures called the double-shuffle, and as time has gone on we have perfected the technique, refining it in ways well known to every Canadian.

The ritual of blackmail is simple and direct. It stultifies differences of creed and magnifies differences of race into fundamental differences, although neither is instinctive or universal. It descries assimilation although the progress of the race has continued that way. Both French and British strains have been derived through a vast congeries of racial mixtures. The French especially have assimilated on a grand scale, with coloured races within their empire, with North American Indians, and certainly, after the Norman invasion, with the Anglo-Saxon. The technique of blackmail deliberately misunderstands the genius of the opposite party, calls in doubt its pieties, and even goes to the length of consciously and deliberately falsifying the history of the other, chiefly in school books for the very young. It consistently builds up a flaming nationalism, beginning with the

49

elementary school, which blesses all that concerns its own race or creed, and damns in detail all that concerns the race or creed of the other. It creates symbols of fanatical loyalty to a false ideal or to an untrue legend—anti-conscription, anti-imperialism, pacifism, isolation, Quebec for the French, Canada for the English, anything will do providing it is mad enough, stupid, vulgar and wicked enough.

The obstacles which prevent us from understanding each other, and standing solidly by each other, are not race or religion or even language. The difficulty "lies in the difference between the things (we) respectively take for granted and accept as matters of common knowledge."

Sir John A. Macdonald saw the difficulty but he thought he could depend upon the native good sense of the people. "We have strengthened the General Government. . . . We thereby make Confederation one people and one government instead of five peoples and five governments." Sir Georges Étienne Cartier affirmed the same belief: "We are of different races, not for the purpose of warring against each other, but in order to compete and emulate for the general welfare."

The principal difficulty has been that neither of the principal parent races has approached the other and invited a common conference upon the needs, interests and ambitions of each other. The result is, that the French declare they desire only to be left alone, to possess full equality, equal rights, and the privilege to survive. When you pin the French down to a definition of any of these seemingly simple and obvious ambitions, the definition becomes vague and the goal elusive. The English desire precisely the same things, including the right to survive, yet the English apparently are as averse to defining their aspirations and goals. But every now and then, and with increasing frequency, both collide and resume the vague phraseology of racial rights and privileges, of quotas and *postes,* and so on. In order to hold a racial or religious group together for social or political action, and make it a hammer in the hands of its masters, it is absolutely necessary to have a symbol that includes every prejudice, fear and ambition. At the present moment this rallying symbol is the nightmare word Conscription. To the English-speaking Canadian it means equal sacrifice for equal privileges, a democratic system that makes no favourites. To the French it means the whip of the majority, the symbol of domination, the command of the conqueror, against which it is necessary to oppose every atom of their resistance. The problem can never be solved in time of war. It can now only be solved in Canada by a generation or two of peacetime education.

The French cannot isolate themselves from the English until they have power to force them out. The English cannot isolate themselves from the French, or disinherit Quebec from the Dominion. We are committed to nationhood, and there is no place for isolation of any sort except the final and profound and irrevocable isolation of the grave. Any talk, therefore, of a French and Catholic Quebec or Peace River, any glib nonsense about a Protestant and English Ontario or British Columbia, is silly and suicidal. If the French should insist on a race-religion Holy Land, and build up a French bloc throughout Canada, it would mean that in another generation there might be one hundred French members in the Federal House. If that bloc were used by fanatics, isolationists, and the flaming nationalists which seem determined to create a new Islam in Canada of race and religion, then of course a nation would become impossible, for the English-speaking population, and not merely the English, would learn the lesson of isolation in their turn and build a bloc to barricade their rights, privileges and destiny. English leaders in our Parliament have shamelessly used the Quebec bloc for wicked ends, and the French vote has too often been a species of blackmail. Should the English become a minority, it might conceivably happen that they in their turn would become *bloquards,* and obtain special privileges by their own adaptation of the blackmail technique. It works both ways, but whichever way it works the end is mounting fear and hate and ultimately death. There is still time, but not a great deal, for the enlightened leaders of both peoples to save the day.

V

A CANADIAN PEOPLE

CONFEDERATION was made by man, and will be revised or scrapped by man if it stands in the way of man's progress. There is no use in wishing or in platitudes about the *bonne entente* or in any form of pretense whatever. There is, however, desperate necessity in understanding just what the British North America Act of March 26, 1867, means, and was intended to mean. It is a federal union in a sense, "a supra-national union in which the heretofore sovereign states surrender part of their sovereignty to the supra-national government . . ." (Humphrey). To make this possible the respective leaders of the joining Provinces gave their consent on the understanding that certain rights and privileges should be guaranteed. French civil law was to prevail in Quebec only. French or English were to be official in the Quebec legislature and in the Parliament of Canada, and French was to be used if desired in Canadian courts of law, but nowhere else, in no other Province. The system of protecting Public as well as Separate schools operating under Ryerson in Ontario was to prevail in Quebec, and so became law. Special provision was made for perpetuating Canadian connection with the Mother Country, and of following the model of the British constitution "so far as our circumstances will permit."

I

The wide variety of powers vested in the Provinces, and the possibility of vast differences in provincial legislation, held the seeds of ultimate disunion, and even of anarchy. It was conceivable that a separate Province might secede; that it might decide to remain in the federation and determine the pace and even the character of the rest of the nation; or that it might use British connection and protection during the years of growth, and when strong decide to withdraw on issues which the rest of the nation regarded as paramount. Coercion would be impossible, a Cullodon or Gettysburg unthinkable. And yet a Province might decide that the issue at stake was not its concern, and nullify the will of the majority. That way, of course, lies national disruption and death. It suggests a total lack of reality in thinking, a failure to recognize the fact that the time might conceivably come when the other Provinces would act in concert in such a way as to destroy the non-cooperative Province, rather than permit that Province to dominate to the harm of the state forever.

"Well aware of the sentiments of our people, I will strive my utmost against a government which has the barefaced effrontery to call itself the protector of the minority. The minority are untrue to their citizenship when they segregate themselves from their fellow-subjects in order to secure privileges for themselves only; and thenceforth they are no longer entitled to the protection of the laws, unless the people of this country are so far demoralized as to lie down submissively at the feet of the few, which I do not believe."

(Louis Joseph Papineau)

In the end the warning of Papineau must prevail or else we shall disintegrate and become a pitiful people. Nearly every Canadian family, of whatever language or faith, came out to Canada to escape poverty or vassalage of some sort, to escape insecurity, age-old animosities and deep-rooted wrongs, to escape into a vast, free, new world on the frontier, where a new nation was in the making, a new people compounded of all the people, the whole vast, rich amalgam of inheritances of them all. It was to be a land of hope, of new enterprises and fresh beginnings, everything washed away by the sea change except what was good and worthy to endure. The race was to be a new thing under the sun, a free and happy assimilation of all the peoples, and the language was in time to be the symbol and idiom of a new way of life, neither wholly English, nor entirely French, neither Ukrainian nor Dutch, for it would grow in time into the perfect expression of its creators. Legends, folk-tales, turns of phrase, handicrafts, all these would become the common property of a resourceful and independent and strongly individualized people.

II

In such a nation there can be no glib talk about the peaceful conquest of Provinces by minorities. Most Canadians are Canadian before all else, and they are the ones who will give Canada whatever place in the sun it deserves. They do not take their orders from London, neither do they take their ideologies from Moscow. They do not shift with the varying diplomatic breezes of Washington or Paris. This does not mean that for profoundly practical reasons they do not

desire to maintain their place in the British Commonwealth, or remain in the orbit of American nations. It
simply means that wild talk about minorities trying
to conquer the world through deathless prejudice has
no future. It means that the spate of silly twitter
these recent war years about men refraining from
fighting and saving their skins to fight again another
day at the ballot box, while their wives work overtime
filling the cradles, will look very weird in time. Some
future historian of Confederation in Canada will come
upon such statements as the following, and there are
not a few of them, and he will marvel that so young
a country could succeed against the wild rhetoric of
these fevered doctrinaires.

"One can understand—without excusing—the Tory
grudge against French Canadians when one considers
our peaceful conquest of the Eastern Townships during
the past fifty years.

"The *Bulletin des Agriculteurs* began some months
ago, the publication of a series of fine reports on the
Province of Quebec by Mlle. Gabrielle Roy. Of singular
interest is that in the last number which treats particularly of the progressive settlement of our people,
in the Eastern Townships.

"Mlle. Roy has found her type of peaceful conqueror
at Moe's River, not far from Compton. An honest
farmer explained to her the transformation which took
place little by little under his eyes. The English and
the Loyalist Yankees sold their land one after the
other, and always to French Canadians. The general
aspect of the land has not changed, the houses have
kept their Anglo-Saxon character and the roads their
ancient trees. But the parish, *la paroisse*, has spread
over and, as everywhere else, the communal life is
organized around the Catholic church spire. This is
what has happened:

" 'This little village now has seen the departure of most of its old faces. The people no longer call themselves Matthew, Bill and Smith, but Baptiste, 'Sidore, Elie. And they work the land, after the fashion ordained for that district, with a patient fidelity which should make it rich and good of its kind. They continue there, after so many have gone.

" 'One fine morning the Protestant minister found himself with almost no congregation at his service. In truth, he wakened to find himself almost without followers, save those who slept their eternal sleep in the sad little plot surrounded with grey stones and, since these did not hear his homilies, he was sad.

" 'Perhaps he took a long walk that day, alone, about the little village which had changed its habits, its customs, its language, and out into the country where he remembered so many vanished friends. Perhaps he reflected long on the reversals of history which carry to attentive hearts the lessons of wisdom and of understanding. He must, after having walked far, have seated himself beside the road and felt descending upon him, more heavily than usual, the evening dusk. But no doubt there lifted before him to console his solitude, the vision of a small and peaceful parsonage . . . someplace in Ontario.'

"Elsewhere, in the west and north of Ontario, our people are tranquilly pursuing their peaceful conquest, making no noise about it, and paying no heed to political theories and nonsense of that sort. They want nothing to do with a 'racial leader.' They have character and they do not fear work. They will conquer." (Quoted by *News* from *Le Canada*, 1945.)

Over against that we may place the following by Jean-Charles Harvey in *Le Jour:*

"Nous savons que nombre d'étudiants et collégiens égarés par des professeurs imbéciles et ignorants, ainsi qu'une poignée de journalistes logés à l'enseigne du fascisme et du corporatisme, ont suivi avec fureur l'étoile de fer-blanc qui s'accrochait aux lèvres des candidats du Bloc. La plupart d'entre eux sont honnêtes et bien intentionnés ... comme l'enfer. J'éprouve à leur égard une sympathie réelle, car je sais que ces jeunes ont subi une terrible déformation et cédé à des influences qui imprégnaient toute la sensibilité de leur âge. C'est pourquoi je voudrais leur dire: 'Ce n'est pas tout de parler de la race et de la langue, de ressusciter les cadavres historiques, d'ergoter à l'infini sur les injustices, réelles ou supposées, de la majorité canadienne, de haïr tout ce qui n'est pas catholique et français. Non, ce n'est pas tout. Il faut vivre, compter avec les voisins, s'adapter au fait accompli de la grande réalité nord-américaine, éviter l'isolement racique; il faut savoir que trois millions d'hommes perdus dans un océan humain de 140 millions de population, ne peuvent se suffire à eux-mêmes; il faut enfin penser en humain avant de penser en laurentien, réfléchir, agir, créer, commercer, produire, échanger . . . O jeunesse, jeunesse! Si tu savais jusqu'à quel point on a abusé de ton honnêteté même, de tes élans vers l'idéal, de ta touchante crédulité! Si tu savais combien on a voulu user de toi comme le chirurgien use des cochons d'Inde, jamais tu ne retournerais vers ces faux guides qui t'ont plongée dans l'absurde de la tête aux pieds!' "

Some of his compatriots call Harvey a renegade, a traitor to his race and other things, but we believe that only through such good sense as he has shown through the years will a Canadian nation be possible.

The Abbé Arthur Maheux has made a veritable apostolate of good will between French and English peoples in Canada that must bear good fruit in time. It is difficult for an outsider to understand the invective levelled against him, the bitterness of it, the malevolence and frightening rage of it. But in the end reason surely will prevail. These are problems which our French neighbours themselves must and will solve. It calls for the best leadership French Canada has produced in all its history. It seems to demand, before all else, the leadership of the French Catholic Church, which in times past, in dreadful moments indeed, has risen so magnificently to point and lead the way.

III

Other races and faiths in Canada must know for certain that the voices of reason and good will are not dead in Laurentie. French and English, we have wronged each other in grievous ways, but the greatest wrong we can ever do our peoples is to perpetuate the memories of these instances of bad manners, bad feeling, badness in many forms. Surely that way lies utter chaos and annihilation. Into the record should go the eloquent words of Major the Abbé Armand Sabourin, chaplain of Les Fusiliers Mont-Royal, upon his return to Canada after D-Day. His words have the greater weight because he took part in the epic invasion, and risked his life with his soldier compatriots that civilization might be saved, and that Canada might be made one in common sacrifices.

Nous nous sommes battus pour le Canada

"Mesdames et messieurs, vous vous demandez peut-être ce à quoi nous pensions en traversant la Manche. A qui nous pensions? Nous pensions à vous, mes chers compatriotes, nous voulions vous éviter à vous les horreurs, des bombardements; nous voulions vous éviter, à vous, que demain, la guerre vienne chez vous; nous voulions empêcher qu'Hitler vienne demain, chez nous, détruire notre foi, notre langue et nos institutions. Nous n'avons pas traversé la Manche pour nous battre

59

pour l'Angleterre, mais nous pensions que nous allions nous battre avec l'Angleterre pour le Canada. Ne me faites pas dire ce que je ne veux pas dire. Je ne viens pas de dire que je n'aime pas l'Angleterre. Je dis que nous nous battons avec l'Angleterre notre Alliée.

Haine de l'Angleterre!

"Pourquoi n'aimerais-je pas l'Angleterre? Parce qu'elle me permet encore de réciter mes prières à genoux tous les matins? Parce qu'elle me permet de dire la messe tous les matins dans mon église? Parce qu'elle permet que dans nos écoles les religieux et les religieuses enseignent le catéchisme? Parce qu'elle me donne la liberté, tous les ans de faire mes processions de la Fête-Dieu dans n'importe quelle rue de ma ville et de mon pays? Parce qu'elle me donne la permission, de grand coeur, parce qu'elle me laisse ma langue, mes écoles, parce qu'elle me laisse toutes mes traditions?

L'Angleterre gardienne de nos libertés

"Voyons, mes chers compatriotes. Eh bien! je vais vous faire un acte, une profession de foi encore plus grande. En ce moment je préfère infiniment être un sujet loyal à l'Angleterre, je préfère infiniment plus que ce soit l'Angleterre qui veille à mes libertés, que d'être sous la tutelle de n'importe quel autre pays du monde dont je n'exclus pas même hélas! la France. Je sais comme vous, mesdames et messieurs, qu'à la tête du gouvernement anglais,—je m'excuse auprès de mes frères protestants,—je sais comme vous que le gouvernement anglais est protestant. Je le sais. Est-ce votre faute si vous êtes catholiques? Est-ce leur faute s'ils sont protestants?

"Laissez donc la Providence faire ce qu'elle a à faire, mais je ne veux pas m'enlever de l'idée que si j'ai toutes mes libertés dans mon pays je les dois à l'Angleterre. Je préfère infiniment plus en ce moment, malgré que le gouvernement ne soit pas de foi catholique, j'aime encore mieux être gouverné par des anglo-protestants, que d'être sous la tutelle d'un Hitler, sous la tutelle d'un Mussolini ou sous quelqu'autre tutelle que ce soit parce qu'alors l'Anglais protestant me laisse, à moi, Canadien français, le droit et la liberté entière de pratiquer ma foi, de parler ma langue et de garder mes traditions. C'est pour ça que nous sommes allée à Dieppe. . . .

Heureux de l'honneur d'avoir été choisis

"Pour Dieppe, je suis le plus heureux du monde qu'on ait jeté les yeux d'abord sur les Canadiens, et le plus heureux du monde qu'on ait choisi les Fusiliers avec plusieurs autres régiment anglais. Ils nous ont donné, à Dieppe, une leçon d'unité. Ils ne nous ont pas dit, le matin de Dieppe: 'Mais comment se fait-il qu'il y ait des régiments canadiens-anglais avec nous?'

"Nous devrions être seuls, les Canadiens français, pour aller à Dieppe. Non, mesdames et messieurs, ce matin-là ce n'est ni le Canada anglais ni le Canada français qui allait vous défendre à Dieppe, c'était le Canada tout court. Et nous sommes partis comme des Canadiens. Marchons donc la tête haute comme Canadiens français. Soyez aussi fiers des vôtres, Canadiens anglais. Soyez fiers des vôtres, Canadiens français. Pour vous épargner les horreurs de la guerre, voilà pourquoi nous avons consenti volontairement à nous rendre, au risque re notre vie, à Dieppe."

IV

Any section of the nation that refuses to become a full partner in all the nation's work, in war or peace, will atrophy and die. Any nation that declines to become a part of the council of enlightened nations leagued to prevent war, and guarantee the benefits of peace, will be left behind to wither and perish. It is written in the stars that people concerned only with their own ailments and wrongs, their own interests and rights, are doomed. Nature spews them out. The fanatical parsons, the crack-pot priests, the slimy friends of the people, the mandarins of the proletariat, and all the imbecile demigogues that set home against home and people against people, these will merit the odium of history as at present they merit the disgust of every decent Canadian.

That there are differences between our Canadian national groups there is no use in denying. Sumner Welles in his *Guide to the Peace* (1945) speaks of the English and French in Canada as follows:

"The English-speaking Canadians are more like Americans than any other people. In national wealth and standard of living, in industrial investment and efficiency, in manner of life in the city and on the farm, the two peoples are closely akin. But Canadians are not Americans—far from it—in spite of cafeterias, drug stores, ice cream sodas, hot dogs, movies and comics. They are a distinct nationality in form American, certainly British, but above all Canadian— shapers of a new culture, convinced of their own national destiny.

"The French Canadians are another story; they add another flavour to that new culture and national destiny, but at present, except for an assimilated minority, they are a people within a people. One may observe the best of their world, which centres in the St. Lawrence region of Quebec, in the novel, *Maria Chapdelaine,* the antique French speech, which knows none of the cultural or political moods of France since 1763; the village clustered about the church with its priest; the songs, the folk-lore, and artisanship of old France; the love of the soil, despite laborious summers and long winters; the many children, the hospitality, the Arcadian indifference to the hustling, material-minded North America about them. There is another side to the picture—remains of illiteracy, less robust children, poverty, intellectual retreat—but these things seem irrelevant to people whose treasure on earth is farm, family and faith."

It is useful to have these observations from those outside our country and looking on in kindness at our experiment in nation building. What we can not tolerate, or ever permit, is the segregation of our two main ethnic groups around antagonistic symbols of domination. If the French, for example, see in Toronto the New Jerusalem of the United Empire Loyalists, or the Holy City of Ultra Toryism; if the English see in Quebec the Mecca of Gallicanism, in Montreal the seat of the Dalai Lama of Laurentianism—then the sooner we destroy the heresy the better. We have seen what "patriotism at a price" will do for a strong proud state, for France, how a nation was tortured by party madness, and how charlatans thrived on tragedy and confusion and division.

Let no one imagine that our English-speaking population can make smug faces at the French. The stupidity of the English in Canada is historic, almost cosmic. If the French in Canada favoured Franco, and preferred the emissaries of Marshal Pétain to De Galle, the English on the whole entirely misunderstood the nature of the struggle in Spain, completely missed the portent of the business in Germany and Austria, and helped slit the throat of the League when our representative asked that teeth be put in sanctions. The Dominion was being led by English-speaking Canadians, and they vied with each other to hoodwink the French in Canada about obligations of all the people, plutocrat and plebeian, in time of war. It was the English who created the "No Conscription!"

terror, and it has plagued them. And all for a solid Quebec vote! Listen once again to these pro-consuls, representing all parties, in the Canadian House of Commons: "We stand resolutely against all participation in imperialist wars." Meaning going to war with England. "We should make up our minds that *never* so far as we are concerned, will we let our sons go across the sea to war again." "I refuse to participate or assist in war . . . we have to keep out of the affairs of Europe." (1934-1935) "In the event of war, Canada should remain strictly neutral, regardless of who the belligerents may be." (1937) "In my opinion our British connection is our gravest danger." (1938) "Canada should be prepared to defend her own shores, but her assistance should be limited to economic aid, and must not include conscription of manpower or the sending of any expeditionary force." (1939)

The mayor of a French metropolis on the eve of war declared that, if Canada were one day to find herself at war with Italy, then French Canadians would be found on the side of Italy against England. Societies and newspapers in France were doing their best to compromise the Republic and whip up animosity against Great Britain, and in French Canada fascist groups were hindering co-operation at home and sowing the seeds of animus against England. But a high Protestant churchman stated publicly at the time, that if he were in Germany he, too, would join the Nazi party. In our universities and peace societies and liberal groups the Empire became the butt of ridicule, the visit of the King and Queen the object of derision, appeasement and isolationism and pacifism at all costs the correct thing. Extreme groups in

Canada, taking their political and economic opinions from an organization far from these shores, swung today this way and tomorrow swung that, with Russia and against England, with Russia and for England, until reason and honour had died of confusion. The degredation of democracy in Canada was almost completed.

Let English-speaking Canadians remember that most of this nonsense, this amazing treason to decency and truth, was conducted in English. The Jews in Europe and the French in Canada have for too long a time been the scape goats for the stupidities and sins of others.

v

Closing a lecture at Queen's University, one of a symposium on *French Canadian Backgrounds,* Senator L. M. Gouin had this to say:

"What do French Canadians want? We want to co-operate with you in maintaining and developing Canada as a free self-governing Dominion, one sovereign nation with two distinct nationalities; a truly bilingual country where the offspring of the first settlers are able everywhere to learn and to speak French; a Canada possessing a true national unity, where Canadians of all creeds and of all origins realize that they are all the sons and daughters of the same mother Canada, their only country; a Canada united physically, yet, but above all, possessing one national soul."

Will any one tell us what is wrong with that? Will any one say that it is not the goal of all intelligent Canadians, French or English, native-born or immigrant? Will any one declare that for such obvious ends as these all of us should, when need arises, be expected to give all, all treasure even unto life itself? Is it to be agreed that one group will, when war comes, dig up a bogus tradition and hide in the deep woods of racialist rhetoric, while others bleed away whole families to the last son? Will we not agree that this is a leaders' problem? That it was our leaders who created it for the most tawdry political purposes, for solid and blindly prejudiced majorities? That they alone can undo it? Will we not resolve, in fact, that they shall do it, and so heal the terrible wound they created and kept open and festering and maggoty for decades? Lay gauleiters and church fuehrers, little ward heelers and big shots, pallid parsons with no gospel except prejudice, grubby party hacks, the very scum of the earth, all of them the vermin of civilization, English and French—and all for a day of drunken power and a shoddy kind of glory. Away with them!

VI

It must be admitted that isolationism has spread rather rapidly and ominously in Quebec during recent years. There is no use in blinking the fact that the rest of Canada fear it, and do not always believe the apostles of the *bonne entente* when they declare, that this noisy separatism is a passing phenomenon, the result of a few noisy boys, and that 95 per cent. of the Province is for a solidly knit Canadian people. There are too many who say that Quebec is a state within a state, that it is a French and Catholic nation in its own right, and that outsiders are there through suffrance. These same people declare hotly that all of Canada is their natural home, and that privileges they

66

enjoy in Quebec must be theirs to enjoy anywhere in Canada. But you can't call a man stranger in Quebec and neighbour or brother in other Provinces. You can't speak of English as the language of heresy in Quebec and say the same thing to an Irish Catholic in Manitoba or a German Catholic in Saskatchewan. There are many entrances into the temple, but there is but one High Altar, and he who rants of language as the symbol of faith, not only forgets the real meaning of the Cross, but is a fool besides.

Canada, as a part of North America, is committed to an American way of life, an American brand of democracy, an American outlook upon other nations abroad, and in time an American language. America is determined that there shall be no Balkanization in the northern half of this hemisphere. It makes no difference where we came from, France or Ireland, Iceland or the Ukraine, in time, sooner or later, there will be an American speech, and it will be our mother tongue. Perhaps the basis of it will be English, since 150,000,000 speak different kinds of English now. What matter? It will be a living thing, growing, expanding, swelling with the life within it. It will be the language of American trade, of American arts and letters, of American life as a whole, and of any and every sect or faith that makes its home on American soil.

VII

"The destiny of mankind is not decided by material computation. When great causes are on the move in the world, stirring all men's souls, drawing them from their firesides, casting aside comfort, wealth, and the pursuit of happiness in response to impulses at once awe-striking and irresistible, we learn that we are spirits, not animals, and that something is going on in space and time, and beyond space and time, which whether we like it or not, spells duty."

(Winston Churchill)

The French Canadian boasts that he has been here three hundred years. Some families no doubt have been, but surely they are not more Canadian than many English speaking families who have been here five and six generations. Both are emancipated from the old world, independent, vassals of no one. To many French the Statute of Westminster (1931) was a farce, and complete freedom was never achieved. But freedom is in the mind; it is in believing oneself free. Nearly every Anglo-Saxon you meet, and practically every New Canadian, knows himself and his children to be free Canadians. Flag and national song will follow—when we can agree on a design, and on tune and words. However, if there is going to be a considerable minority shouting: "Our French State, we will have it!" what's the use? Who then will be Governor-General? What the national anthem? The flag? In French constituencies one frequently sees the flags of France and of the Pope flying from mastheads and fluttering from windows, and rarely the Union Jack or the Canadian Ensign. In the rest of Canada there is little or no observance of either national or holy days with flag or ceremonies. No one is to blame and no one to be censured so long as the country can not make up its mind to unite and be one Canadian people. But we shall get along much faster if we do not start swearing at each other, and waving Papal flags, Soviet Russia flags, the flags of France or Eire in the air, the air that is already so cluttered and confused and stormy.

Parliament, that has given us so many lessons in the art of slander and animus, in the mobilization of fear and greed for party purposes, has also in enlightened moments shown a better way.

Speaking in the House of Commons at the height of the conscription issue, the Prime Minister stated the case for all our people for all time.

Task of Parliament to Safeguard Unity

I cannot believe this parliament is going to permit that unity to be destroyed by a political quarrel over a question of the method by which men are to be raised for overseas service. Canada, and Canada's future, is far more vital than any question of conscription. It is not for me to tell any hon. member how he should proceed in presenting the issue to his constituents. I do believe, however, that the issue of conscription for overseas service would soon vanish from the realm of political controversy if those who prefer conscription for service overseas would say to their constituents: "There are thousands of patriotic Canadians who, for reasons that are readily understood, are opposed to conscription for service overseas and that we should be prepared, at this time, to take those reasons into account"; and if those who are opposed to conscription for overseas service would say to their constituents: "I prefer the voluntary system and I will do my utmost to make it work, and I appeal to you to do the same; but, if conscription is ever needed for Canada's sake and for Canada's future, I will not oppose its application."

Both might say to their constituents: "We are fighting this war as one free and united people against an enemy who seeks first to destroy our unity so that later he may take away our freedom and our country itself. In the face of that terrible danger, we cannot afford to have any differences that it is at all possible to avoid."

In the whole history of the world, no two peoples have ever lived so long in such close association with so little friction as those of French and British descent in Canada. In a century of political union we have built a nation which stretches across half a continent. We have conquered the wilderness. We have achieved great material progress. We all have become deeply attached to one common homeland. We have accomplished miracles in order to help defend our homeland against a ruthless enemy. No one will ever make me believe that in the hour of testing, the achievement of a century is to be imperilled by permitting any issue to arise which might threaten our national unity, and that in the hour of its greatest danger and in the time of gravest crisis for all mankind.

The Right Attitude

Lest words of mine might appear to be biased or exaggerated, I should like to quote from an editorial which appeared in the Montreal *Standard* of May 30, and which is entitled "Crisis in Canada." It is but one of a number of editorials which have recently appeared in publications throughout Canada, which sense with clearness the real danger to Canada, should the right attitude not be assumed at this time by all whose responsibility it is to guide our country's present course and help to shape its future destiny. It presents an appeal which I believe will meet with a ready response in this House of Commons, and which I also believe expresses the true spirit of Canada. The editorial reads as follows:

"The Dominion of Canada stands at the most critical hour of its history. Its future as a nation depends on understanding between English and French-speaking Canadians. One cannot make Canada without the other. At the present moment there is a grave danger of a cleft being driven between the two that would not close over for generations.

It is not a political situation, a crisis of corridor and caucus. It is a crisis of feeling. And a nation's life depends on the feelings of its people.

Only if there is a strong will for understanding on both sides can we come through the difficult times that have arrived. Canada must come first in thought, in action and in words.

English-speaking Canadians must force their minds to understand the background of the thinking of their French-speaking compatriots. They must realize that their fellows in Quebec are intensely loyal to Canada, that they hate the enemy and his works as much as anybody, that they have contributed mightily to the country's war effort. English-speaking Canadians must realize that the hard fact that Canada is fighting for her own survival in this war has not been brought home to French-speaking Canadians and that the lack has been intensified by words and actions not truly Canadian from many individuals; that there is a long history behind the recently expressed opinion of French Canada. They must guard against giving too great weight to extreme elements in Quebec.

French-speaking Canadians in their turn, must grasp that the mass of their fellow countrymen are thinking of Canada, its safety and its future, are not putting other considerations above that of their own nation. They must understand the perils that beset their country, and realize that it is better to keep those dangers as far away from our own shores as possible. They must have forbearance for those who are prejudice-bound on the other side, and see that the feelings of the majority of other Canadians are fundamentally as their own.

If the will to understand does not grow on both sides, Canada is heading into disaster. If the will swells on both sides, Canada will play her full part in beating back the enemy that seeks her life, and will be assured of a future as a nation worthy of the two great peoples, each retaining their own strengths, united to form a whole that will be an example to the world."

VIII

Protected behind the Munro Doctrine and the British fleet, we have bred a weird type of limited liability citizenship. There is a section of our people that curses the United States only a little less violently than Great Britain, totally unaware of the source of our security, totally ignorant of the hard fact that we can not protect ourselves, and never shall be able to do so independently of any foreign aid. The highway between both Europe and Asia, swept by the swarming shadows of armadas of the air speeding round the world, we are in a fair way to become another Plain of Esdraelon, valley of battles of those contending for the life-lines of world power. It is high time, therefore, that we recognized our friends, our most dependable and strongest allies, and bound them to us by every enduring tie. We shall find that military alliances for mutual protection, no less than trade agreements, will pay splendid dividends, and that in time of danger the total mobilization of wealth and manhood for the preservation of our rights and freedoms will pay best of all. There is no other way of being a friend and neighbour. There is no such thing as moderate friendship in time of calamity, or partial sacrifice, measured interest, among true allies in time of war. "The essential basis of attachment is ideological, related not to the tradition of blood, but to the tradition of national institutions and spiritual inheritance." (A. Brady)

The English mobilized the Canadian French to help save their empire in America. These Canadians were for the most part feudal and without skill in democracy, and were natural defenders of a Tory regime, and even of an Empire party. When injustice crept into England's treatment of her new wards in Canada, it was Burke and Fox who cried out for justice and decency, and their names deserve to stand by that of Governor Murray as champions and saviours of the young French province. Humanity and decency are not dead. There have always been strong men to defend our French neighbours. We shall make more rapid progress in reaching an intelligent entente if we recognize, that the French have not emerged as far as other Canadians from feudalism, and from ways of life that are not democratic in the full modern sense of the word. It is too late now to say that differences in historic backgrounds separate us, unless we have memories that go back three hundred years, and are determined to dwell there. If our residence in Canada as neighbours for 150 years means nothing in building common grounds for united action, we are poor trash. We are headed into a great democratic experiment, a North American democracy, and everyone must move with the times, move onward and move together, or be tossed aside, as blind, deaf, dwarfed, misshapen, unusable.

IX

Many have regretted that the United Empire Loyalist tradition in Ontario and the Maritimes has been almost totally forgotten. It stood for an attitude toward Church and King that became the backbone of the infant state. In time it stood for privilege, for smugness, for callous indifference to the rights of others, for a deadly feudal regime in government, church and education. There were some splendid things about it, nevertheless, but English Canadians have tended to suppress the whole tradition, knowing, in their hard practical way, that in the end too much of it would make a total mess of nation building. The English may have a natural talent for democratic government, but it requires a lot of buttressing and fresh inspiration and constant checking to make it work, for while the talent may be native and natural the practical achievement of democracy is far from a spontaneous growth. To hear some journalists and politicians speak about Tory and Loyalist Ontario you would suppose we were back in the days of the Family Compact. Nothing could be a greater mistake.

If English-speaking Canada is determined to grow up politically, anxious to slough off the impediment of its colonial past; if New Canadians are willing to leave behind all that can not be readily assimilated into the new Canadian life; then Canadians east and West, French and English, Slav and Jew, must honestly and courageously pledge themselves to minimize those things which keep up apart, and strengthen those things which tend to bring us together, and by all and every means fight the enemies of democracy in whatever form they appear. The future is for free men, and nothing can be withheld from them if they march together as equals and friends.

For the present, to speak of unity seems to spell disaster to our French neighbours. They prefer to call it solidarity. They dread absorption and oblivion as French speaking people. In the end there can be only unity. Generations ahead, what happened in Great Britain after the Norman Conquest must eventually happen here. Whether the whole people speaks French or English, or a rich dialect compounded of both, with many imported words, and including folk idioms born out of the amazing inventiveness of America, it does not matter. Surely it does not matter! The language of England is not the language of Caedmon or William the Norman, and who knows what it will be another millenium hence! Let us face facts, then, and let us confess that in the end nothing matters but man himself. Let there be an end to the irresponsible and capricious speech of certain of our leaders, who say that the French labourer is a mere cog in the conqueror's industrial wheel; that the Pope is trying to run Canada; that the French are tools of a scheming priesthood that owns them body and soul; that the English-speaking Canadians are scraped from the very dregs of the vat of Great Britain for the purpose of overwhelming the French. Saracen or Christian? It all sounds utterly mad, completely unreal!

We have made a wretched fetish of the number of years we have resided in Canada, French and English. Length makes not a jot of difference in the final claim of rights. It is the quality of the living that counts, the completeness and intelligence of the living that matters. My family were among the nationalists of Southern Ireland, and shed their blood so late as 1916 for a free Irish State. But why should I or my children import this hate of England, this frenzy, this passion for the folk lore of Cuchulain, and for the epics of the warrior chiefs of Butler and Ormond from whom we are said to descend? Why revert to Erse and furbish the memories of old wrongs and cruelties?

> Out of Ireland have we come.
> Great hatred, little room,
> Maimed us at the start,
> I carry from my mother's womb,
>   A fanatic heart.

(W. B. Yeats)

The Pope aided William of Orange in his campaign against Ireland, but who remembers that on the Glorious Twelfth? A British government, for generations opposed to the Papacy, and forbidding the enthronement of a Roman Bishop in its realm, nevertheless paved the way for a Bishop of Quebec, and in shorter time than the first Bishop was enthroned under the Most Christian and Catholic King of France. He who dwells in the past should know all the past. It is an exceedingly mixed business, and one should be cautious in accepting any of it without reservations. Would it not be better to think, that out of it emerge certain great traditions which become the landmarks of all the peoples, and that the rest returns to dust? Would it not be better to believe, that the present demands all our thought and care, and that those who try to keep one eye on their dynasty or age-old prejudices or past wrongs, crying out for revenge, and the other eye on the exciting business of surviving unchanged in a swiftly revolving world—that they are doomed?

X

The fundamental fact of Canadian federation is, that at bottom it is a spiritual enterprise. To build a

76

personality at all requires the betrothal and ripening of all the inner powers and interests of a man. One does not move blandly and unconsciously into full maturity as an individual, but only by taking thought, and by infinite pains. It requires some attention to the family and tradition out of which one has come, and in the state this is preserved in the arts and letters, the history and folk tales of the race. In a sense these provide the continuity. But for the rest it is an individual matter, finding oneself, being oneself, quietly but firmly being resolved to fulfil one's own destiny, supply one's own needs in one's own way, come hot come cold, come rain or shine.

Democracy is such an achievement. It requires time and much ripening in all weathers. There are those who affirm, that even the Christian way of life can not be achieved in solitude and by prayer alone, but rather that full-orbed Christian living needs life at the full, the meeting and sharing of many people, the wrestling and the withstanding and the overcoming. It is upon such a venture we are all launched, and it calls for a higher kind of leadership than any we have yet had.

It seems clear to many that, if a man is to get anywhere, he must work out for himself a goal of some sort, the higher the better—and the sooner the better also. The more one delays that decision the longer one postpones becoming mature, and one can not arrive anywhere until one ripens and hardens into a person with a purpose.

So, too, this business of making a nation here. We must take aim. When we have done that, then the melting pot, immigration and assimilation, and all the rest, will have settled down to where they belong in the scheme of things. We can not hold this vast Dominion against the land-hungry world. If we wait for our own natural increase to people it as it should be stocked, we will find the crowded nations moving in without our permission. And why not? Canada will support, on a decent standard of living, at least five times its present population, and the resulting conglomerate will be neither French nor English—but Canadian. If we can get it into our heads, that vast areas of Canada remain to be peopled by permanent, self-sustaining plantations; who will care nothing about French or English traditions as such; who will be indifferent to the hates of warring sects unless priest and parson stoke the fires; who will be honestly ambitious to make a living here for themselves and their children, to become Canadians, and defend their homeland and the kind of life they have evolved for themselves, whether the enemy strikes here or abroad —if we can once clearly see this, then our big battle is over.

The trouble seems to have been that we have had no national calamity in Canada. We have had no crises that shook the nation, demoralized it with tragedy, and made all else trivial. A people that has passed through such a crucible has a history, a birthright literature, drama and art, songs, flags and heroic traditions—all are born in pain. For the lack of a great fusing fire, we go on bickering over the possibilities of the melting pot, the ascendancy of this race or that, the percentages of jobs available in public services, and the relative sacrifices of principal nationals in times of war. We set up Switzerland as a model for states within states.

If we have French and English states within Canada, why not a Hebrew state, or a Slavic state? If Canada must accommodate itself to a noisy and intransigeant minority, then can not the Jew bide his time and demand, by the force of numbers, economic power, control of newspapers, radio, motion pictures, drugs or tailoring, a place in the sun? Switzerland is not a nation in the true sense. It is a compromise, a truce, an incorporated company. It has no arts and letters or any personality usually associated with independent and autonomous states. It survives as a curiosity, and is permitted to survive because the world apparently requires an international postal address, first aid station, rest house, no-man's land. A lot of nonsense is spoken about Switzerland as a model for Canada. A people is either one or it is two; and if it is two then it is on its way to join the dodo.

XI

There can be no Confederation if there is to be a religious test. There can be no Confederation if races persist as races. There can be no Confederation if it is more honourable to preserve a traditional way of life than to enter wholeheartedly into the living, throbbing life of the present day. There can be no Confederation if democracy is invoked in peacetime and flouted in war; if races and religions blast out special privileges through blackmail in times of stress and tragedy. There can be no Confederation if one language is regarded as the voice of heresy and the other the voice of God; if literature is made the vehicle for all that is inflammatory in history, and history is made the custodian of all the remembered

79

wrongs and humiliations of the past. There can be no Confederation if schools are not free, free of the pressure of politicians, free of the blight of religious fanatics, free as all outdoors to search for truth and honour it when found. There can be no Confederation if lodge and sect, labour union and board of trade, party and race deliberately foster prejudice.

The people know this. Thousands of men returned from the last war determined above all to be Canadians, but were sickened to death by the divisions they found. How could so small a people survive when stricken by so many sundering forces? Why, of course, they could not! And now their sons are returning, old and wise in many ways before their time. No country ever looked so good, so lovely, so utterly wonderful and desirable! But what of tomorrow? Those who are not blind can see something coming, something almost cosmic in its elemental force. Those who will to live in the past, or in an ivory tower, will be by-passed and forgotten. If they get in the way they will be swept aside. What is solid and good and usable will survive, the rest—the little, mean, racial, religious, priggish, stupid, dispensible things—they will take themselves away, or be crushed. New books will be written, new orations will be given, school courses devised, marching songs and banners proposed, and all will end at the ballot box. The old charlatan will have a hard time. The bogus friends and shoddy leaders of the people are in for a beating. Men want work, and they want time to play, to live seven days a week, and they will have it. And the Top Men, architects of the new day, may be Roman Catholics or Protestants, of French or English or Polish extraction, it doesn't matter a hoot. There will be no racial or religious prejudices unless subsidized parsons and professional friends of the people keep the fires burning. In time the people may realize that peace at home, as well as survival, may well depend upon these wild men being taken out and hanged.

XII

This is no time to twitter about the balance sheets of our mutual mistakes, French and English. We have both sinned dreadfully. This is no time to talk nonsense about the first citizens. He is first who stands first, be he black or white, Christian or Jew. This is no time to snuffle about quotas of jobs; it is a matter of aptitude, training, qualification, and that rests with each man himself. It all comes back to me, am I good enough, wise enough, kindly enough, anxious enough to join hands and move ahead? If not, then you will not be to blame. It is not a question simply of tact, though God knows we could stand a lot more of that happy lubricant. We need simple honesty more than anything else. We know deep down that we act like wretched idiots in our pawing and scratching at each other, but few have the honesty and courage to step back and laugh. Rather do we hide the truth under elaborate discussion about the place of regionalism in our arts and letters, under absurd academic huffling about the virtues of provincialism and the benefits of parochialism in this and that. We evade the issue by stating that time passed us by, and prevented us from participating in this liberalizing movement, in that fructifying event, when the truth is that we evaded change, novelty and progress as we shunned Satan

81

himself. The old way was restricted, but it was comfortable, and one knew where he was at so to speak! The fault is in ourselves, not in our stars. Jean Charles Harvey once wrote:

"There is one contribution French-speaking Canada could make right away to the cause of national unity which would in no sense run counter to the basic traditions of our nationality. We used to be one of the greatest pioneering races in the world. Practically the entire continent of North America, if we except the Atlantic coastline between New England and Florida, and the Pacific states and provinces, was discovered and opened to civilization by men from what is now the Province of Quebec. But the qualities of daring, initiative, and endurance which were so characteristic of early French Canada are not being applied today to the equally difficult, equally taxing problems of modern progress, because nothing has been done to call them out and train them in the light of changed conditions.

I am convinced that the establishment of an adequate, practical system of education in French Canada would soon prepare our people to resume, in the fields of industry, trade and finance, the pioneering role they once played in the opening of the North American frontiers. The lapse of French Canada into defeatism, into exaggerated sensitiveness, in to a sort of inferiority complex closely resembling that of the Old Testament Jews, is comparatively a new thing in Canadian life. And it is a thing superimposed deliberately upon our people by inventors of all sorts of philosophical, political, and educational shibboleths who have themselves lost sight of the realistic aspects of the struggle for survival in North America."

Yes, the fault is in ourselves, and not in our stars, or in the army of ragamuffin leaders that contend for our souls. These scarecrow prophets will have their little day and cease to be. There is nothing sacrosanct in Anglo-Saxony. There is nothing inviolable in any race under the sun. There is nothing holy or sacred about religion, any religion, that prostitutes itself for tawdry ends—fostering prejudice, kindling racial animosities, organizing social and economic forces for silent war against neighbours of other faiths, using all the skulduggery of the cheap ward boss for the purposes of secular power.

The fault is in ourselves. We know when we are being poisoned. We know when we are being hood-winked. And we are divine to this extent at least—we know when we have had enough! There are certain people who are doing all they can to destroy any good the war may bring us out of the terrible crucible of common suffering of mankind. There are certain elements in Canada who are resolved with a kind of blind madness to heap the fires of prejudice, both racial and religious, and let loose a conflagration. There are ministers of religion so black as to egg us on to the verge of civil war. There are national and provincial leaders who would send us back to the jungle, who manipulate minorities with all the cunning of savages and all the cruelty of wild beasts. Out upon them!

The days ahead are full of portent. They demand all our resources of intelligence and good will. Few countries are so splendidly endowed as this, so vastly worth the effort. A great and noble future is ours, providing greatness and nobility are alive in us and in our sons and daughters. Canada! Even the name is beautiful, a portent, a promise to her people and to the world. She awaits the leadership of the new élite, those who have passed through great suffering, who have made expiation in these terrible years, who have grown wise and kind. These are the chevaliers of the new Canadian Legion of Honour. These are they who honour and defend one another, who place every other reward or distinction below that of promoting the unity, well-being and happiness of this fair, dear land.